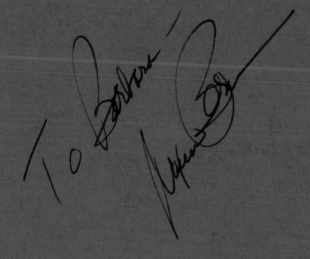

To Barbara

THE ONLY
BOOBS
IN THE
HOUSE
ARE
MEN

THE ONLY
BOOBS
IN THE
HOUSE
ARE
MEN

**A VETERAN WOMAN LEGISLATOR
LIFTS THE LID ON POLITICS MACHO STYLE**

MAXINE BERMAN

Momentum Books, Ltd.

Manufactured in the United States of America

1997 1996 1995 1994   5 4 3 2 1

Momentum Books Ltd.
6964 Crooks Road
Troy, Michigan 48098
U.S.A.

ISBN 1-879094-34-7 Paper
ISBN: 1-879094-33-9 Cloth

To my mother...
For her love, patience, and encouragement.

TABLE OF CONTENTS

ACKNOWLEDGMENTS

This book wasn't easy to write. Shortly before it was acquired by the publisher, the Michigan State Legislature, bless them, went on a wacky tax cutting spree, leaving no money to open schools in 1994. I was one of fourteen people in the 110 member Michigan House designated to repair the damage.

So I would first like to thank the rest of the Fabulous Fourteen for pumping my adrenaline during the week to such high levels that it never lowered much on the weekends when I really needed it to write.

Many others deserve special thanks:

My family and friends, for sticking with me, even-though they almost never saw me during the process.

My loyal, long-suffering legislative staff, Michele Slocum and Ron Hicks, for putting up with me and for taking up the slack when I desperately needed it.

Gerry Feder, for helping me with some of the more subtle complexities of my computer, like how to turn it on.

Shirlee Citron, for her help in editing.

Bill Haney, for his editing wisdom and his faith in publishing this book.

Ann Beser, for taking me on a walk through Arlington National Cemetery.

The men of the legislature. What can I say?

And most of all, the women of the legislature. Just for being there.

INTRODUCTION

Several years ago, one of Lansing's male political correspondents asked six women legislators to do an interview about what it was like to be a woman in the legislature. Four of the women chaired important committees, our expertise ranging from appropriations to election law to retirement to education. The reporter had only two questions: Did we think the lavatory facilities were equal, and did we feel obligated to always wear dresses or skirts instead of pants?

Ever since that remarkable experience with investigative journalism, I have often thought that one of us really should tell our story. It isn't an easy thing to do. As much as we are a distinct, separate minority, we are also part of a whole. Perhaps more so than in any other job, collegiality is critical. Telling the truth risks ostracism or a cement block tied to the foot of our political careers. We have to go along to get along. So women legislators remain silent, even though they may seethe underneath.

When we get together for lunch or dinner, the real stories tumble out. Sometimes, we laugh so hard at our male colleagues that we can barely eat. Sometimes, we seriously finger the table knives. No matter whether we serve in Congress or state legislatures, no matter which part of the country or state we're from, the stories are the same. And then we go back to our legislative chambers and become part of the team again.

I have always tried to be a legislator first, part of the team, and I think I've generally succeeded. But it is impossible not to be a woman legislator simultaneously. Many of our male colleagues make certain of that, not simply by sexist words and deeds, but by greedily—some might say hysterically—clinging to all the good stuff in the legislature, offering us a world of supply-side politics, trickle-down power.

It's probably hardest for first-term women to understand. How many times have I heard new women colleagues say it?: "Spare me the 'women's issues.' Lead me to the economy or the environment or insurance. Lead me anywhere else." But hard as any woman may try to avoid it, pigeon-holing by gender is insured by most of our male colleagues' absolute unwillingness to carry the lead on any issue with which they cannot anatomically identify.

So we become experts on insurance law *and* pay

equity, on utility regulations *and* prenatal care, on national defense *and* family leave, on small business regulations *and* child custody. And no matter how much credit we deserve for the nongender-related subjects, we become best known for "women's work." After all, the press can ask a man about everything else.

In addition to being mentally and physically draining, our double duty on some issues, like choice, sex education and family planning, often pits us against America's right wing. Then we become known as radical feminists. So the cycle continues: our critical work on behalf of women was left to us because of sexism and our efforts in these areas inspires more sexism. The office makes the feminazi.

In spite of it all, I really don't mind the double duty. My six terms in the Michigan legislature have given me the opportunity to affect people's lives, to broaden my vision, to meet wonderful, exciting people of both genders, to play an important role in what happens to my state. Also, more than anything else in my life, they have taught me what it really means to be a woman. The lessons haven't always been easy.

So this is my version of the world, my notes from under the dome, way under. It is a story that belongs to all of us.

(Oh, by the way, the lavatory facilities have only recently become equal and sometimes I wear Levis.)

[1]

PMS:
POLITICS—
MACHO STYLE

In Anglo-Saxon times, a nobleman formed a group of warriors around him in an exclusive relationship known as the *comitatus*. He chose them to protect his lands and acquire new ones; they chose him to protect their lives and acquire status in their own realms. The symbiosis became known as the spirit of the *comitatus*: a special relationship of absolute, to-the-death fealty and archetypal camaraderie.

Aside from the nobility itself, the men who formed the *comitatus*, or *comites*, shared the highest rank in feudal society and constituted the political and social leadership of the community. They were combat ready. They controlled everything. They were men.

Surely, the lesser endowed aspired to the feeling, if not the rank, of the *comitatus*, eventually forming various associations like guilds. And so the notion filtered down. Other men were men too! And their sons were men. And their sons were men. And pretty soon in America, they joined things like football huddles and unions and chambers of commerce. And they were all men too.

And a select few, the actual political descendants of the *comitatus*, became the Congress. And they were all men too. Except that, apparently due to the shortsightedness of the country's founders, there wasn't enough room for all of them. So the rest of them became state legislators. And when those positions filled up, they became city councilmen and county commissioners. And because all of them had to protect their personal turf, their modern day feudal estates, they formed their own *comites* to insure their continued success and celebrity. And those were called political parties. And together they formed other *comites* to finance their needs. And those were called PACs.

The spirit of the *comitatus* remains quintessentially male. That instantaneous identification, that locker-room/barroom savoir-faire is local, national, global, and it can contract or expand at any given moment. For example, the white *comitatus* rarely acknowledges the black *comitatus* until an emergency crystallizes the need. Enter Clarence Thomas. And all of them acknowledge each other when they become sports fans. So the size of the group can be fluid. If you're a man.

Not if you're a woman.

As newly elected legislators, my first-term colleagues and I were feted at numerous receptions thrown by various interest groups. It was not uncommon for a man who had never seen me before to "chivalrously" take my hand and kiss it or plant a light peck on my cheek. I could not help but notice that this was distinctly different from the glad-handing, backslapping welcome-to-the-club received by my new male colleagues. Mutual philosophical concerns had nothing to do with my acceptance by the group. For the most part, after almost six terms in the legislature, that's still true.

Were these circumstances peculiar only to those areas outside the House chambers, the psychic gulf could be set aside. Unfortunately, that is not the case: the spirit of the *comitatus* is directly responsible for the number of women in Congress and state legislatures throughout the country. For instance, women, like all nonincumbents, gain easiest access to elective office when an open seat exists. Yet over half of today's congressional delegation was not in office ten years ago and the number of women in Congress moved only from 4.5 percent to 10 percent. In the Michigan legislature, 59 percent of the people I began serving with in 1983 are gone, and some seats have changed hands many times, yet the number of women has risen only from 10.8 percent to 19.5 percent. Women have captured only 16 percent of the eighty-seven seats vacated.

The people who make the difference in gaining entree to political office—men—literally perpetuate the difference. They move uncontrollably toward people who look like they do and shrink uncontrollably from those who don't.

Women who have been lucky enough to break down the barriers and enter this enchanted land soon find that the political chasm translates into issues. Most men simply assume that it is our job to handle things like prenatal care, child care, breast cancer. (There actually is no such thing as a "woman's issue." Women care equally about the economy, roads, insurance, national defense, etc. Some issues just aren't men's.) The only time these men wrest a "woman's issue" from us is when there is a fetus involved.

And when abortion threatens to tear apart legislatures, the fault lies not with increasing societal anxieties but with elected women who demand to be heard on the subject. In Michigan, these debates used to last no more than five minutes, with one man standing up for each side to offer a pious statement. Now they last five to seven hours. Our presence simply wreaks havoc on the spirit of the *comitatus*.

Men are never angry with the men who invariably introduce legislation to restrict abortion rights, but they are furious with us for making them uncomfortable—and sometimes for missing lunch: "Hey, you're screwing up the process! Don't you know the rules?!" In fact, as I write this, a group of four men, one pro choice, three not, are meeting to debate what to do about the latest bill to undermine abortion rights in Michigan. Pro choice women have been specifically excluded from the discussions. There is no womb with the ins. It isn't just our positions on the issues; it's our unwillingness to go along with their process. We might break the spell or code, or both.

Many men are suspicious of us not simply because we are there, though that's probably bad enough, but because they apparently believe we have our own *comitatus* that they don't understand or accept. I'm not sure they're right. I don't know if there is a female *comitatus*. This is not to say that almost all of us don't share some form of identification, but it is often an identification based upon being left out, rather than being part of a particularly familiar circle.

Frankly, almost the only time I ever feel part of the legislative *comitatus* is at the annual legislator/lobbyist softball game, which I volunteered to take over when no one was looking. We're rarely invited to the men's lunches or for drinks after work (though it's okay for male legislators to bring their wives). This game allows legislators to let their collective hair down, to find a commonality with each other that can be critical in negotiations on the floor. Mostly, of course, I just do it because it's fun. But for one brief "shining" moment, my female colleagues and I gain access to and share at least a modicum of the *comitatus*, including the after-game beer and pizza at a local watering hole.

And you know what? Now that I've done it a few times, I must tell you: they don't talk about anything. Even when they think they're talking about something, they're not. They just shoot the breeze and it's usually a warm one. Which doesn't mean it isn't fun. But it does mean that the medium of the *comitatus* is the message they cherish, whether they know it or not.

In *Cat's Cradle*, Kurt Vonnegut introduces a granfalloon: a group of people who find an instant identity, a permanent relationship, based upon the most irrelevant of grounds. "You're from Ohio! Hey, I'm from Ohio too!" "You went to Penn State! I went there!" "Hey, you've got a penis! Wow! Me too!"

The *comitatus* lives.

[2]

POLITICS, PACS
AND YOUR
MAMMARY GLANDS

I'm not a doctor, but every year dozens of women call me with questions about breast cancer. Some of them have already been diagnosed. Frightened, angry, and exasperated, the women who call all make one mistake: they view breast cancer only from the perspective of a patient. They would be far better off if they also viewed it as a consumer and a voter.

Breast cancer treatment is big business. And where there is big business there is politics. And where there is politics there are PACs. And where there are PACs there is influence. And all of these elements are controlled by people who do not have breasts.

It all started in the 1960s and 1970s when women like Happy Rockefeller and Betty Ford did a tremendous service by openly discussing their mastectomies. Until that time, almost no one ever admitted having had one.

The revelations inspired a fresh breeze of reality and acceptance. If Happy and Betty could remain "whole" women, so, too, could others who had lost a breast to cancer. Equally important was the message to millions of women for whom the standard breast cancer treatment was far worse than the disease. In many minds, mammography was nothing more than the first step on the road to what they considered the terrible fate of mastectomy.

But when Happy and Betty went public, the light bulb that went on in women's heads lit up in others' too. Open discussion fostered a lucrative industry. By the early 1980s, the once hard to find breast care and mammography clinics were springing up everywhere. In my legislative district, they were as easy to locate as fast food restaurants and video stores: Implants to Go! Blockbuster Mammography!

My first experience with the politics of breast cancer came in 1983 when I introduced a bill requiring informed consent for those diagnosed with breast cancer. Women would have to be told about all available medical options. At that time, a modified radical mastectomy, involving removal of the entire breast, was the pro forma treatment. However, many women were candidates for lumpectomy, removing only that segment of the breast containing the tumor, usually followed by radiation. In addition, many women underwent a chilling one-step procedure: if the biopsy was positive, the mastectomy was done immediately. The patient awoke not knowing if she still had a breast, with no possibility to participate in her treatment decisions at all.

The majority of patients simply went along with their doctor's almost inevitable recommendation of mastectomy. But a few others, mostly younger women, dared to question. Often, they had to approach four or five doctors before they could even find one to tell them about lumpectomy. My hope was that if lumpectomy were more common, and commonly understood, more women would be willing to have regular screening mammography, since lumpectomy is usually only an option in early stage cancers.

I was a naive first-term legislator with what I thought was a simple, straightforward bill which only required doctors to hand patients a brochure explaining all the options. The brochure would be written by the Department of Public Health with the full input of the medical community. In spite of the fact that doctors were not required to favor any of the options, the entire medical community exploded. Who was I to tell them what to tell their patients?

An intensive lobbying campaign began in the legislature. My county medical society even devoted an entire legislative breakfast to it, almost the only one in my tenure that did not center on demands for reforms in medical liability. It was also the only time in my eleven years that I can recall them placing a woman doctor at the head table so that she could describe the catastrophic consequences of the bill. (Another example of what I have always called the Phyllis Schlafly

Syndrome: whenever men in control face women in insurgence, they place a woman on the front lines: "See, not all women agree." That means the rest of the men don't have to pay attention either.)

The only committee hearing on the bill that term was jammed with angry women bearing horror stories and officious doctors bearing big books. The books, scientific tomes on breast cancer, easily weighed ten pounds each. As the doctors laboriously made their way to the mike to testify, their texts turning them into hunchbacks, the message became both implicit and explicit: any woman who couldn't read or understand these books was clearly not a candidate for informed consent. I wondered if they were willing to make a concession for women who could carry them.

In testimony before the House Public Health Committee, the doctors presented a heavy dose of pitfalls:

> 1. The state should not interfere with what we do—ever—period. (This apparently did not count when it came to *their* requests to interfere, as in demanding help with their insurance problems.)
>
> 2. Women diagnosed with breast cancer are too upset to be given options. It would only confuse them. (Can you imagine an argument suggesting that men might be confused by options if there were such a thing as a penisectomy?)

3. This is just a vanity issue. (As if their brothers in plastic surgery weren't salivating in the wings, fanning the flames of the breast implant "miracle.")

4. You're ruining the "love" relationship, as one doctor called it, between doctor and patient. (Given the choice between the relationship and the breast, which would you take?)

5. She might have to travel some distance for some treatments and be away from her children, so I don't tell her those options. (More than one doctor's genuine definition of informed consent, i.e., Father Knows Best.)

6. Lumpectomy is not as good a treatment as mastectomy. (This was the toughest argument to fight, in spite of scattered studies and a few wonderful, courageous doctors willing to buck their colleagues and say otherwise. For legislative men who were looking for a way to extricate themselves from the intense lobbying pressure, it was the perfect place to hang their political hats.)

The real argument went unspoken. Comparatively few doctors do lumpectomy with radiation, and doctors, like everyone else, tend to not like what they don't do or know about. Moreover, if they couldn't do it and had to tell women about it, those women might go elsewhere and somebody else would make the money.

The bill died in committee, the death blow clearly delivered by a statement of opposition from the Michigan Cancer Foundation (not to be confused with the Cancer Society), led by a male doctor who was not about to let his brothers in the Michigan State Medical Society down, no matter what the cost.

When I reintroduced the bill the next term, the Foundation continued its opposition until they ran into a problem. They desperately wanted a tax credit for donations and I had just become chair of the House subcommittee controlling tax credits. It took them over a year to connect the lack of action on their bill to their opposition to mine. Ultimately, I traded them the offer of a hearing in exchange for their silence.

The reintroduction of the bill the next term also received a tremendous boost when it coincided with the publication of an article in the *New England Journal of Medicine* declaring lumpectomy with radiation as every bit as effective as mastectomy when treating early stage breast cancer. The article received national media coverage and many of my male colleagues who had yawned or cowered their way through the bill's first term now rushed to show their support. In their minds, it had become a good "woman's vote," and heaven knows most of them need it.

But there was still the Medical Society, a three hundred pound gorilla beating its chest, not breasts, determined to protect its turf. Until the gorilla came up against a public relations problem. The legislature was in the midst of a year-long battle on liability reform and the

Society was losing points with its position on informed consent. Caps on liability had become far more important than consent on lumpectomy. They would never support the bill, but they would at least shut up.

The bill passed, but I have no illusions about my unique abilities in its success. Were it not for a combination of propitious circumstances, there would still be no Informed Consent for Breast Cancer law in Michigan today. And I have no illusions that passage of the bill, more than three years after its introduction, meant victory. It is, unfortunately, a law that is very difficult to enforce. Finding doctors who are not giving out the required information is almost wholly dependent on women knowing in advance that they're supposed to receive it.

Most doctors apparently follow the letter of the law—why risk a fine or reprimand?—but ignore the spirit, perfunctorily handing out the brochure while at the same time ominously warning their patients that mastectomy is the best treatment: "If you were *my* wife...." A 1992 national study by the American Cancer Society justifies my concerns: less than a third of women diagnosed with early stage breast cancer are treated by lumpectomy with radiation. Michigan's figure, though higher than before the bill's passage, is around 30 percent. Only about twenty states have the law.

The three-year bloodbath over Informed Consent made my proposal to establish strict quality guidelines for mammography look easy. The bill was enacted in six months. By that time, of course, I was in my fourth term and a lot wilier. And I was materially aided by a lengthy expose on poor quality mammography in *The Detroit News* in the fall of 1988. Also, the Michigan Department of Public Health, which estimated problems in 50-75 percent of our facilities (typical nationally), was calling for immediate action. But most important was the powerful and tireless support of doctors of radiology and breast cancer surgeons, i.e., the medical community was split from the start. Further, since few doctors had anything to do with mammography, they had little interest in actively opposing the bill.

Not that that ever translated into support. After all, a few doctors didn't like the bill, especially some general practitioners who were offering mammograms to women in their offices, often performed by nurses or receptionists with no training, often on machines that were wholly inadequate, often read by the doctors themselves, who rarely had sufficient training in radiology.

And then entered the Michigan Hospital Association, a group equally powerful to the Medical Society. They didn't like the bill: "We don't want more regulations. We don't need more inspections. We do it right anyway." (Sad testimony from some women proved otherwise.) And some rural hospitals warned that the requirements might deny women in their area the only mammography easily available—as if it were better to have a bad mammogram than have to travel fifty or even a hundred miles for a good one.

While we made some concessions to the Association, who, of course, sent a woman to lobby the issue, we would not accommodate their primary request to drop the whole idea. In the end, the Association, like the Medical Society, took no position on the bill, obviously too embarrassed to oppose it openly.

Has this law made a difference in Michigan? Absolutely! Prior to its passage, only 5 percent of Michigan's machines were accredited by the American College of Radiology. Today, 70 percent are, with the other 30 percent somewhere in the accreditation process. This is far more than anywhere else in the country. In 1992, Congress used Michigan's landmark model to enact national legislation.

But as in the case of Informed Consent, passage of a law does not always guarantee genuine compliance. Mammography is far too big of an industry to give in easily. For instance, a 1992 article in *The Detroit Free Press* fingered several prominent hospitals for problems with phantom imaging. (The phantom is the device used to determine if the machine can pick up the kinds of problems or irregularities found in a woman's breast.) The backlash from the Michigan Hospital Association was deafening: the problem wasn't with the *hospitals*; the *rating* system was all wrong.

The Department of Public Health panicked. Facing a loss of consortium with one of their most beloved PACs, appointees of the new Governor began shooting the messengers: the state's inspectors of radiologic health. The Department quickly called a meeting for those who wanted to "express concerns" about the law, a meeting which would have never been held had the facilities listed in the paper been small clinics with no political clout.

The packed house at the meeting was more than vaguely reminiscent of the first informed consent committee hearing years earlier. Dozens of hospitals sent representatives bearing phantoms and complex graphs. Apparently, they couldn't find big books to prove their scientific superiority, though they naturally found two women to testify against the department's procedures.

The results? The complex rating criteria was simplified, even though no one was able to explain why this supposedly cockamamie system found imaging problems in more than 75 percent of the facilities in Detroit's tri-county area and almost none in many other counties around the state. One bonus from the uproar was that while many women were frightened by the revelations, thousands of them began calling the Cancer Society to find out which machines were accredited, by far the best way to put the persistent noncompliers out of business.

The other result was that the Hospital Association was even angrier with me than when I introduced the bill. They very pointedly told me how lucky I was that they hadn't opposed it from the beginning, neglecting to mention that they didn't have the votes. And I became *persona non grata* in the Michigan Department of Public Health. But that's O.K. They couldn't ignore me forever: I now chair the committee that controls their budget.

And that's how it works. It is not my issue against your concerns. It is my power against yours. It is my votes against your PAC. It is my grass roots against your sizable political influence. But it is never, never my health or yours and what to do about it.

Women in Michigan even lack the clout, in spite of millions of our names on insurance policies, to make screening mammography a mandated benefit. When I introduced a bill to do that, the insurance industry, corporate lobbyists, labor unions, and even the Department of Public Health formed a rare coalition with a mutual heart seizure. While their concerns were understandable, their priorities remain skewed. There are probably too many mandated benefits in this country which do drive up the cost of health care. But rather than reject screening mammography out of hand, it seems more rational and fairer to review all mandated benefits to determine cost effectiveness and importance. For example, perhaps we could trade off hair transplants (for guess who?) in some states for mammography. Early diagnosis clearly saves lives, but it also saves money. A Wisconsin study proves that, disputing the previous belief that late-stage discovery is cheaper because women die faster.

Ultimately, I had to settle for legislation that required coverage for screening mammography to be offered, not mandated, and there has been some increase in coverage since the law was enacted. But that hardly goes far enough. Offering isn't mandating and self-insured companies are covered by federal, not state, laws. Further, the vast majority of negotiators who determine what is even offered to employees once again do not have breasts.

Knowing that, women will simply have to take charge. Our health may be dependent still on people who do not share our anatomy, but our selection of that health care is totally ours. Women who religiously read the labels on everything at the supermarket will have to start reading the labels of health care in America. Is the mammography facility accredited? Prove it. Which treatment options are available? Is it covered? Why not?

Politically—and *en masse*—women will have to demand better care. We cannot afford to hang separately. We cannot afford to look into a phantom mammography image and find a little PAC. If it cannot be done because it is good policy, rest assured it will be done if it becomes good politics. Because that's the name of the game.

[3]

DEAR JOHN

I recently received one of those off-the-wall constituent letters. What distinguished this one from most of the others was that the man was actually dumb enough to sign it.

The writer claimed that two Washington insiders told him Hillary Clinton was the first First Lady lesbian in the United States. He wanted to know if it was true. He signed it "Seriously, John Smith."

Seriously.

There are various ways to handle a letter like this. The first is tossing it in the nearest trash basket. Another is a standard form letter many of us like to send. It goes something like this:

Dear John,
I think you should know that someone has gotten hold of

your stationery and is using it to send really stupid letters to legislators. Since I would never want anyone doing this to me, I wanted to make you aware of it right away. It's really a shame when we have to keep something like stationery under lock and key, isn't it?

This reply is always sent in an envelope marked "Personal and Confidential."

For some reason, I decided not to let John Smith (not his real name) go without a real answer. So I sent him the following letter.

Dear John,

I have received your letter regarding Hillary Clinton.

Let me assure you that the two Washington insiders are not insiders at all.

It is unfortunate that there are many men in this country who simply cannot come to grips with the fact that many women, married or single, are intelligent beings and capable of functioning at very high levels in both the private sector and government. Because of their own clear feelings of inadequacy, both intellectual and/or sexual, these men feel very threatened by capable women and often find that the only way they can maintain what they feel is their God-given male superiority is to cast aspersions on these more qualified women. One way, of course, is to call them lesbians.

Take the case of Janet Reno. The women who preceded her as potential attorney general nominees were hounded by child-care issues. While I believe many of those concerns were justified, I do not recall any male nominee for any post being questioned about his child-care arrangements. Because Janet Reno is single, child care was not a problem. But because she is single, rumors (probably initiated by the two Washington insiders you know) immediately began that she is a lesbian. She is not. I guess women just can't win.

I'm sure you share my hope that we will some day see a world where gay bashing is no longer a national sport and where women's intellectual capacities and strengths in heretofore less traditional roles do not make them the target of name-calling. This, of course, means that many men will have to look elsewhere to justify their intellectual or sexual abilities. I'm sure strong men will survive.

He wrote back and called me a feminazi.

My staff and I have gotten a few good chuckles out of it, but the truth is that the whole thing is not funny at all. I don't really think the letter writer ever believed that Hillary Clinton is a lesbian, if for no other reason than that he's probably too dumb to think that any lesbian has ever had a child. Yet he was all too eager to adopt obnoxious, often vicious labeling of women.

The abuse seems to be getting worse. It was always there before, but not so open, not so acceptable. There's certainly been an increase since Bill Clinton was elected. I see it in letters and Op Ed pages, I hear it at meetings and on talk radio. While we may be quick to condemn the blatant pornographic abuse heaped on women by Andrew Dice Clay, we seem more than willing to embrace it when people like

Rush Limbaugh say the same thing in euphemism. Part of it is probably nothing more than a bad case of right-wing sour grapes—The Grapes of Rush—but this is the kind of thing that sticks.

As women become more visible in high stakes positions and as the nation's leader supports and promotes them, those who see their status quo lifestyles threatened are bound to strike back. For the average person, the name-calling may be a relatively harmless recreational pursuit. In fact, I'm willing to bet that John Smith would be the first to tell you that he has the greatest respect for women, that he treats his wife like a rare jewel. You know, the kind of man who puts women on a pedestal so that they can never participate in what's going on on the ground floor.

But when this violent verbal backlash becomes habitual in average, dare-we-call-them-sane Americans, what happens to the not-so-average, the not-so-sane? This is the kind of atmosphere that allowed a sick young man to go on a killing spree on a Montreal campus a few years ago, gunning down every woman he saw. I worry about that.

I also worry about the long-term effects on young women, the kind of statistics that are hard to count. If they grow up in a world where competent, successful women are labeled as lesbians or nazis or ball-breakers or anti-family, which career paths, if any, do you think they'll choose? No one wants to be the scapegoat, the outsider, particularly children, who need so much to be accepted. So their bodies will be strewn across America, just like in Montreal, except in this case they'll still be breathing.

I'm not sure how to combat it. The right wing has always been brilliant with words: pro life, feminazi, family values, tax and spend. Countering with words has little effect. We don't seem to be as good at it and besides, it brings us down to their level. Countering with lengthy, logical essays doesn't work either in a country which feeds on thirty second sound bites.

A part of me says to chuck it all, that it's not my problem, not my responsibility. Find another job. Get out of this business. Another part of me says I have to stay for all the same reasons.

Of course, some of my friends and colleagues warn me that if I continue writing the kind of letters I do to the John Smiths of my district, I won't have to decide whether or not to stay in office. I'll simply be thrown out.

But I'm not worried about John Smith. I'm worried about his daughter.

[4]

THE FAMILY JEWELS

A Reader's Guide to the Men of the Legislature

Several years ago, I attended a charity roast of a male capital reporter. All but one of the approximately ten male roasters, most of whom were legislators, devoted their entire "amusing" presentations to penis size. *All but one.* The men loved it.

If it had no other value, the evening confirmed my suspicion that if men were categorizing their male colleagues, their critical physical proportions would be the sole standard.

Needless to say, I have no interest in knowing the "gifts" of my male colleagues. Yet it seems only fair to define the men I work with, especially in terms of their attitudes toward women, in terms easiest for them to understand. The jewelry box was open for view long before I got there.

DIAMOND SOLITAIRES

Perfectly cut gems, they are hard to find and almost impossible to duplicate. Diamond Solitaires are the few truly wonderful men who adorn the legislature with their genuine respect for and equal treatment of women colleagues. Not that we agree philosophically on everything; in fact, we've had some strong disputes and probably find each other pretty exasperating at times. But in legislative work, neither our gender nor theirs really matters to them, and that's all women can ask. Some have become good friends and as good confidantes as any woman I know could be.

It should come as no surprise that the Carbuncles and Cubic Zirconias (see below) find the Diamond Solitaires a little hard to take. The former two groups, far greater in number, often go out of their way to mask the brilliance of the Solitaires. It's not just the Solitaires' willingness to work with and include women, though that's two sins right there, but their self-assurance is very threatening to the less valuable gemstones. Freud was wrong: penis envy is clearly a psychological affliction of men, not women. (I figured that out at the roast. The event wasn't a total waste.)

Now for the bad news: Diamond Solitaires represent only about 5 percent of the legislature.

DIAMONDS IN THE ROUGH

The majority of men in the legislature are really quite admirable in terms of their willingness to work with women, to respect our opinions and positions. It hasn't always been easy, but they have come to terms with the fact that we are there. True, it is sometimes impossible not to notice a telling little shudder when we're around, but they somehow always manage to adjust. While only a few have the potential to become Diamond Solitaires, the rest still produce a true quality glow.

The most interesting men in this category are some of the legislature's senior members who served for years with few, if any, women. Our presence surely remains an anomaly to some, having grown up viewing women's roles differently. One once called me a "sweet young thing." I am none of those three, and I probably should have at least facetiously punched him out. But this senior male legislator has fought for my rights and placement on committees and for that I am grateful. I try hard to make accommodations for the generation gap.

The sad thing about the more senior Diamonds in the Rough is that it took so long to earn their respect and acceptance. After eight to ten years, most women finally become part of the crowd and it's a good feeling. It's simply irritating that we had to wait so long and go through the Bataan Death March to get there. Of course, they've gone through a lengthy psychological battle too, and it's been harder for them than some of the younger men.

Never give up on old gemstones; they can be reset.

CUBIC ZIRCONIAS

Cubic Zirconias are artificial diamonds which like to think they're real, but aren't quite sure. With little, if any, philosophy of their own, these men came into office instinctively looking for the seats of power—the ornate, gold-plated settings to enhance their own value.

Actually, they're pretty funny to watch. Their votes often go up late on the tally board because they're waiting to see how the powerful Carbuncles want them to vote—never mind their constituents. Some are terrified of voting at all. Why, then, run for office? Surely, they never told the people they represent that they wanted to be legislators so they could see how someone else votes first?

Any practiced legislative observer can spot them. If they're not literally hanging on a Carbuncle's shoulders like an off-centered, bespangled epaulet, they're in his office, waiting for cues. An unwitting passerby would probably mistake them for constituents. In a way, they are. After hours, they're at some local bar, listening to their personal talisman, their Lord of the Guys, holding court. They fetch the drinks.

Cubic Zirconias fear women, though rarely hate them. Since the Carbuncles have warned them that women are supposed to be seen (elsewhere) and not elected, they find our presence more than just a little disquieting. I keep waiting for one of them to say, "My Dad said I couldn't play with you. If he finds out I'm talking to you, I'm really going to get it." And he probably will.

I have often wondered whether the problem of these

men is that they don't have the cubic zirconias they were born with—or that their problem is that they do.

Fortunately, Cubic Zirconias represent only about 20 percent of the legislature. Unfortunately, they represent about 20 percent of the legislature.

RHINESTONES

If we were talking about metals here, these poor little guys would defeat the skills of a certified alchemist.

It is amazing they were ever elected. Could all of the boring, barely-clinging-to-mediocrity voters be squeezed into a few legislative districts, looking for someone with whom to identify to elect to office? These are the kind of people to whom Dorothy Parker was referring when, upon being told that Calvin Coolidge was dead, asked, "How can they tell?" The only time the rest of us share anything in common with them is during those long, sometimes twenty-four hour sessions when everyone else is asleep too.

Dully sensing their lack of value, Rhinestones are intimidated by just about everyone in the legislature. However, it's one thing to know that all of the other men are smarter than they are; it's another to know that all of the women are too. Someplace in their alleged minds, they understand that this is simply not the order of things. They can tell that by watching the Cubic Zirconias and the Carbuncles.

Mostly they just snicker at women colleagues, mistakenly assuming their phony glitter fools everyone. For obvious reasons, they are particularly wary of the more aggressive women, pointing out to the few male colleagues who are sometimes trapped into listening to them that we're more masculine than feminine. In other words, we have all of the qualities they desperately want and the only way they can hold their heads up and keep their rhinestones intact is to mock us for it. A snicker is the most powerful gesture these dolts can muster.

PASTE PEARLS OF PIETY

If prayer resolved all our problems, we could break session every day right after the invocation. The Paste Pearls of Piety are probably the only members who take these few daily minutes of solemnity solemnly.

Our Christian fundamentalists are few in number and not very powerful. But they are there. And they do have their very special way of viewing—or shall we saying *judging*?—the women with whom they work.

God has told them to love mankind and they do. But taking the Bible literally, that leaves us out. To them, "barefoot and pregnant" is not necessarily based on a maniacal need for control. It is simply the word of God. The nature of things. The Pearls would kill us off kindly, with religion.

And everyone else too.

The way to tell if a pearl is real is to bite down gently on it and run it over your teeth. If it's smooth and slippery, it's fake. I have heard our Paste Pearls espouse their love for the poor in almost the same breath they used to explain why they opposed allowing homeless people to register to vote. I have heard them espouse their love for the fetus and their abhorrence of abortion in almost the same breath they used to explain why they simply couldn't vote for a bill to guarantee adopted children the same automatic insurance rights that biological children have. As one explained to me, while he thought the bill would help promote adoption over abortion, a situation devoutly to be wished, he just didn't want to do anything to hurt the small private insurers who were opposing the bill. Ignoring women's rights to save a fetus was one thing; ignoring insurance companies' cash flow to achieve the same end was another.

That's why the courtesy with which we are treated by these men, like precious jewels ourselves, constantly polished and wrapped in velvet, is more chilling than refreshing. We know that from the bottoms of their Bibles, Paste Pearls of Piety believe that women have no rightful place in the legislature.

In truth, Paste Pearls of Piety have almost as much trouble establishing collegiality with their male counterparts as they do with their female. They don't "huddle" on the floor. They don't go out for drinks after work. They don't participate in dirty jokes. (We tell a lot of dirty jokes in the legislature. It helps to pass the time while we're decimating school funding or obliterating the environment.) Frankly, I'd much rather hear them tell jokes about screwing women anatomically than watch them go piously about the business of screwing us legislatively.

The reason they can sometimes manage to do this in spite of their small numbers and lesser strength is that they are backed up by the extraordinarily loud, well-organized, well-funded groups who were responsible for electing them. So they are often successful with amendments that they call moral and I call sexist. The amendments scare the hell out of the Cubic Zirconias and Rhinestones and are quickly picked up by the Carbuncles as a way to exert control. Pretty soon there's a whole jewelry box full of suspect gems anxious to clip a studded choker of discrimination around our throats.

CARBUNCLES

I have a necklace with many different beads on it. Since I like some of the beads better than others, when I wear the necklace, I try to position what I consider the ugly beads at the back of my neck so that only the ones I really like will show. The problem is that the beads I don't like are heavier than the beads I do, so as I move around during the day, the heavier beads inevitably slip toward the front. The shift not only hides the nicer beads, but tugs the whole necklace and me out of shape. This is exactly what happens with the Carbuncles.

A carbuncle is a type of garnet, the blood red gemstone. It is also commonly known as a skin sore oozing pus, sexist sores on the body politic who, while few in number, want nothing more than to tug women legislators out of shape and out of office. Having yet to come to grips with the fact that a House is not a Home and a Woman is not a Wife, Carbuncles view the phrase "woman legislator" as a contradiction in terms.

Unfortunately, Carbuncles tend to be some of the heavyweights in the legislature. If they weren't, who would care?: they'd just be Cubic Zirconias. Few have any leadership titles. Why bother with ornate medallions pinned to their chests when they often run the show anyway? If they avoid titles, they don't have to assume responsibility or explain anything to the press. If they need something done, they simply send the Cubic Zirconias scurrying around the floor to do it.

Some have been known to refuse to take up a female colleague's bill in their committees, even if they like the bill. (Of course, they always offer a different public rationale.) That would be admitting we have a right to be there. Worse, it would be admitting that we're *colleagues*. Some of them refuse to participate in meetings where women members are present. Why negotiate anything with a nonentity? It's how they get their carbuncles off.

While political philosophy did not determine membership in any of the categories above (except for the Paste Pearls of Piety by default), the majority of Carbuncles are conservatives. And almost all of them instinctively oppose a woman's right to choose, an issue which goes far beyond many of their genuine religious convictions. Women who are allowed to make their own decisions on something as important as terminating a pregnancy might think they have a right to control their own destiny in everything else too, like running for office.

Those of us who lock horns with them on this issue are singled out for special wrath. Most legislators who disagree with each other on an issue are able to put aside their differences when the debate is over and reunite to work on other matters. This is even true of Paste Pearls of Piety. That's how life works in the legislature. Today you may be my enemy, but tomorrow I may need your vote.

None of this applies to Carbuncles. Their lines are drawn in cement. Pro choice women are clearly out of control—their control. To them, iron control is all that matters. Abortion is a mere subset of that.

It should come as no surprise that Carbuncles are almost always senior members who came from an era that genuinely believed a woman's place was solely in the home. I suspect these men love their wives and daughters deeply, but that they long ago established a clear pecking order within their own households. (It is tempting to call it The Order of the Pecker.) Like the Paste Pearls of Piety, they have absolved "their women" from all responsibility, from all worry, from all major family burdens. "Their women" are like expensive ornaments, locked away in a safe deposit box, to be taken out only for special occasions, like parties, cooking meals, giving birth. But when women become ornaments with no responsibility, no worries, no burdens, they also have no input into decision making. Ergo, no rightful place in the legislature.

The Carbuncles' throwback attitude might be forgivable if they didn't share it with many of the Diamonds in the Rough who were ultimately ready to accept the new reality. Apparently Diamonds in the Rough have enough self-esteem to compensate for our presence; Carbuncles clearly don't.

Perhaps women should just ignore the Carbuncles. I ignore other distasteful people in politics and it's pretty easy to disregard Cubic Zirconias, Rhinestones, and Paste Pearls of Piety, especially when you know what the real thing is. Unfortunately, Carbuncles not only exert influence on many of the other family jewels, but often on legislative leadership as well and that entails influence on the legislative agenda. It can be pretty hard to work in pus up to your ankles.

It would be nice to think that if we wait long enough, they would all just die out—literally. The problem is that the Cubic Zirconias are standing in line to take their place in the legislative string of beads and when they do, these artificial little mutants won't have any idea why they should be vile, obnoxious sexists. They'll just know they should be.

Life, as they say, oozes on.

And all of the legislative jewelry keeps slipping along with it.

[5]

WELCOME
TO THE
LOCKER ROOM

I borrowed a staff member's daughter to participate in "Take our Daughters to Work Day." The day was designed to raise the self-esteem of young women, to expose them to many kinds of occupations, to let them know that their horizons are limitless. During the preceding week, I spent a lot of time thinking about what I should say about my job.

Should I tell her that she should set a goal to run for the legislature?...

—Because you can make a difference and effect real change in so many issues that will probably be neglected if women aren't in the legislature: women's health, child care, equal rights, and who knows what else by the time you come of age. And you can help prove our worth in all areas by becoming involved in a broad range of issues.

—Because political power can be a pretty heady thing, and there is no better feeling, no greater high, than when one of your bills is enacted which really improves people's lives.

—Because you'll mean so much to so many people who often find women more accessible than men, and you have a responsibility to speak for those who have no voice.

—Because your visibility will make you a role model and may help ease the way for women in many other fields.

—Because it is an honor to serve and very few are lucky enough to do it.

Or should I tell her that running for the legislature should be crossed off her list of future options?...

—Because your agenda will always come last, if it's even considered at all. And if the public ever becomes interested in that agenda, it may be snatched away from you and somebody else—a man—will get all of the credit for all of your work.

—Because you will be denied any position of real power. Even when men are forced to deal with you—after all, you do have a vote—you can tell that they're usually looking right through you.

—Because you will often be pushed into

corners until you are forced to lash back, at which point you will be accused of being a radical feminist or a victim of PMS. You will be viewed as a sweet young thing or grand-motherly, depending on your age; wishy-washy, a bitch or a ball-breaker, depending on your reactions.

—Because being a role model can be terribly draining and women's groups, in particular, will unwittingly do their best to burn you out.

—Because in terms of the prestige of serving, you should remember that old story told by Abraham Lincoln when asked what it felt like to be President. The story was of a man tarred and feathered and ridden out of town on a rail. When asked about his treatment, the man answered, "If it weren't for the honor of the thing, I'd just as soon walk."

My decision came down squarely on the negative side on the morning of "Take our Daughters to Work Day" when Michigan newspapers gave wide coverage to an incident that occurred in our esteemed State Senate. A young woman reporter, Jennifer Van Doren, had written a column in her university paper about interviewing State Senators Jack Welborn and Gil DiNello regarding DiNello's bill to ban topless dancing.

According to Van Doren, Welborn's response to her question was to turn to DiNello and ask, "So, how's that DiNello titty bill going?" DiNello lifted his jacket lapels and laughed, "Well, they're still here."

This was bad enough. But when criticism mounted after Van Doren's column appeared, Welborn and DiNello, who would have been considered neanderthals in the Pleistocene Era, refused to apologize. DiNello accused Van Doren of "political correctness crap" and said she should spend less time on the trivial and more time on important bills like his.

Welborn took the issue to even greater heights. He owed no apology because "Tit is not a sensitive word to me; I'm a dairy farmer." (We all really *do* look alike, don't we?) Later he said, "That's what happens when you let girls into the men's locker room."

So on "Take our Daughters to Work Day," this was the atmosphere, the men's locker room, into which I brought Danica, age ten, to spend the day with me. The "titty affair" was the major topic of discussion in the Capitol and spilled over onto the Senate floor during their session.

Danica and I skipped the Senate and went first to a budget hearing. Next we attended a lunch for all the young women and their sponsors and heard talks from women legislators, lobbyists, and staff so that our guests could see the wide range of opportunity in government work.

Finally, we attended the House session and I let Danica press my voting button for me on dozens of amendments on a controversial bill. By this time, we had made a connection, not simply because of the time we'd spent together, but because we discovered a mutual interest in basketball. Danica loves the game, plays on a team, and knows all about every major college and professional player in Michigan.

I love the sport, too, and told her I played when I was in high school. But that was when girls were only allowed to play half-court basketball, with each side fielding their offensive and defensive players against the other team's on each half of the court. Apparently we were considered too weak to run the length of the floor, or perhaps they just figured we'd be too stupid to remember what to do by the time we got to the other basket. And there were no regular teams. It was just gym.

By this time, I had really warmed to the subject and talked about the recently completed women's NCAA championships. I said I looked forward to the day when there would be a professional women's basketball league. I told her I hoped that it would be there for her if that was what she wanted.

At this point, I noticed Danica glaring at me, her chin jutted out the way only a ten year old can do. "I'm going to play on a *men*'s team!" she scolded me. God bless her. I'm getting old; she's not.

My mood and my outlook brightened; memories of Senators with half-court brains began to fade.

I told her to run. She'll make a great addition to the men's locker room.

Move over, Senators. We've got a live one coming.

[6]

CASA NOSTRA

Our House—and its Rules

In *The Cider House Rules*, John Irving describes a set of rules to live by—acceptable behavior standards, literally posted on a wall near a light switch where they can't possibly be missed. The problem is that all of the people to whom the rules apply can't read, don't speak English or just ignore them anyway. Quintessential Americana.

In the legislature, the situation is reversed. While we have lengthy written rules governing floor and committee procedures, the men's rules to live by are not posted on any walls. Ignoring all the written rules near the light switch which women foolishly take to heart, male colleagues just seem to pass down their own maxims genetically from one term to the next. This makes it particularly difficult for those of us who lack a Y chromosome.

But it's fun to watch anyway.

Rule # 1: WE ALWAYS DID IT THAT WAY!

One of the hardest things about being a new legislator is that you are dropped into an arena where everyone has a history but you. In this regard, senior members can be particularly helpful in guiding first-term colleagues through issues: when and how to bring them up, which are easier, which are doomed at the start. This is called institutional memory.

But WE ALWAYS DID IT THAT WAY! has nothing to do with institutional memory. It has to do with institutional turf. If you want to play in my backyard, I get to run the game.

During my first term on the Appropriations Committee (by which time I was beginning my ninth year in the legislature), I suggested that part of our very tight budget problems might be alleviated if we stopped padding budgets allocated for hiring department employees. The truth was that few of our departments were utilizing their full, budgeted staff and a hiring freeze made it impossible to bring in more anyway. We could use the money elsewhere.

One of my male colleagues on the committee immediately countered my suggestion with "WE ALWAYS DID IT THAT WAY! I've been here nineteen years and WE ALWAYS DID IT THAT WAY." He felt no need to offer any further rationale. Why bother? Had he been in the legislature for only one year, his reaction would have been the same, since the key word to focus on here is *"We."*

I made the mistake of answering my nineteen-year

colleague with "So what?" "So what?" is not the correct response. The correct response is "Oh."

Rule #2: WE NEVER DID IT THAT WAY!

This is a natural complement to Rule #1. When the legislature creates a new board or commission, for example, we often delineate in statute the types of people who will serve on it. This generally includes geography, sometimes race, sometimes professional qualifications or interest group affiliation. Not gender.

Several years ago, one woman colleague, working in committee on just such a bill, listened to her colleagues speak expansively about the importance of getting a good demographic mix, one which would really reflect the state. "We want to be as inclusive here as possible," one male committee member sermonized, clearly including himself and everyone who looked like him, no matter what other qualifications they might or might not have. The woman committee member suggested, only half facetiously, that if they were truly interested in mirroring the state's citizens, they should also use gender demographics. "WE NEVER DID IT THAT WAY!" came the response from her otherwise all male committee—immediately and in unison. It's not that they opposed having women on the new commission; they simply opposed the possibility of having more than one, and if history were to repeat itself, which Rules #1 and #2 prove it must, there probably would be only one woman.

Our problem is that when women aren't spelled

out, they're left out. My colleague keeps trying.

But by far my favorite example of Rules #1 and #2 came on my second day in the legislature. The Speaker called a Democratic caucus. I was ecstatic: This was it! This was the big time! This was the power meeting! This was the most in of the in things to do!

The state was facing an enormous deficit. The year before, we had been in the humiliating position of asking for a loan from the Japanese, the very people who were helping to decimate our automobile industry and therefore our state. This caucus would clearly begin the strategy for the state's turnaround. I couldn't wait to get there.

The entire "Welcome to the Big Time" caucus was spent arguing over whether secretaries should have to punch in and punch out for work on time clocks or just enter and leave the building unannounced as they always had. One full hour of WE ALWAYS DID IT THAT WAY! or WE NEVER DID IT THAT WAY!

Looking back, it might have been one of the most interesting caucuses we ever had.

Rule #3: KEEP IT IN THE FAMILY!

The Mafia has its code of silence. They have nothing on the legislature.

As in any other occupation, lawmakers try to protect their own to the extent they are able, except this goes far beyond professional protection. For all legislators, silence can be particularly difficult when a colleague uses eyebrow-raising tactics to get something done. For women, it can be particularly stressful when it becomes a matter of revealing blatant sexism, which may hamper our ability to do our job. So we just tell each other, and in talking about it, we get even madder. But no one tells it loud enough for outsiders to hear. If we did, what good would it do? There are no civil rights protections for relationships between supposedly equal legislators. Telling not only risks more sexism in retribution, but a potentially negative reaction from our constituents, who did not elect us to office to win victories in the battle of the sexes.

On another plane, KEEP IT IN THE FAMILY! means keeping disagreements within a caucus within the caucus or keeping state problems in the basement files of government. No one is supposed to know that we're not all one big happy family or that there's a dead body rotting in a trunk downstairs.

A few years ago, one of my male colleagues, who was apparently genetically deficient and didn't know the rule, quietly circulated his own auto insurance reform plan, a plan different than that being devised by his caucus leadership. The mere circulation of the letter suggested something was awry in the caucus plan. It took him over a year to get back into the good graces of the Speaker. The legislator who somehow intercepted the relatively privately circulated memo and buried it in the family again by turning it over to the Speaker was the happiest person in the House for weeks. Who wouldn't enjoy having his ears and neck scratched?

KEEP IT IN THE FAMILY! also entails smoothing

over problems in the state, if not covering them up outright. At this point legislators resemble many of those glittery names on charitable board letterheads. You know—the professional donors who aren't really interested in the charity and are happy as long as they get credit for caring about it and no blame when things go wrong. Those who expose problems are betrayers of the family, absolute traitors, potentially shunned for life. Under these circumstances, who would tell? Sometimes, the entire legislature becomes a letterhead.

So what's the result? People may suffer in terrible conditions in some adult foster care homes because many legislators believe that's better than letting the public know that the government people in charge of overseeing them aren't doing their job. Or the state may continue to fund a highly suspect company or group because that's better than losing the support or vote of the legislator in whose district the dubious recipient resides. KEEP IT IN THE FAMILY! has gotten so out of hand nationally that most legislatures, including federal, were forced to enact whistleblower protection laws. It's a sweet—and convenient—irony that these laws generally apply only to private or nonprofit groups, not the governmental bodies that passed them.

The need to KEEP IT IN THE FAMILY! presents male leadership with something of a quandary: they have to include women members, lest we might tell. These are the times when we are suddenly the beneficiaries of the back-slapping, one-of-the-boys rituals usually reserved for our male colleagues. I often hear myself saying, "You mean me?" On these occasions, women become much like baseball players picked up at the end of the season to help the team in its final stretch run to the pennant. Often, these players are brought in too late to qualify to play in the World Series, so they are no longer useful when the good part comes.

I know the feeling.

Rule #4: FIND OUT WHO TOLD!

This is a response to breaking Rule #3. Most men spend far more time trying to figure out who exposed something than they do trying to fix the problem. That's one of the reasons the Tailhook incident took so long to resolve. The Navy was far more interested in getting to the bottom of who told in order to save their own bottoms than it was in punishing the offenders. In the typical male mind, if no one tells, there is no offense.

When the Anita Hill controversy became public, the nation argued for months over whether she was telling the truth. In the meantime, the Senate spent much of its efforts trying to uncover the person who leaked the story to the press. Perhaps that's why they looked so idiotic during the hearings. Their collective minds were simply someplace else, on what they considered the *real* offense.

If the press did as much investigative journalism as everyone presumed—and wished—they did, uncovering the squealers might be easier. Since the legislature, if no one else, understands that "investigative journalism" can be loosely translated into "praying for a leak," elected officials feel they must immediately start tracking down the culprits within their own legislative bodies and staff.

And what happens when the leakers are caught? The Mafia treats its traitors to a sumptuous meal and then slits their throats. We don't do that. We skip the meal.

Rule #5: DO IT AND PRETEND YOU DIDN'T.

It is a commonly held belief among many male legislators that they should never have to explain their votes...of course, some of them truly can't. For a few, this is simply a matter of arrogance. For most, it is the definition of political survival. Apparently, if the vote isn't explained, it never happened. (This is closely related to the rationale for Rule #4.)

In 1983, when the legislature passed a desperately needed income tax increase to save the state from bankruptcy, legislative leaders calmed the more hysterical of the colleagues they talked into voting for it by assuring them that the issue would simply go away. Just find the nearest table and dive under it for a little while, they suggested. Like good lemmings, many followed their leaders.

Bad timing: the advice was given during an explosion of the tax revolt movement in Michigan, so the first place angry citizens looked was under the table. There they found two State Senators who ended up being recalled. This situation might not have happened if legislative leaders, who have easiest access to press ears, had given a full accounting of the state's problems. On the other hand, legislators who did spent a lot of time explaining the details of the fiscal crisis to their constituents came through the upheaval pretty much unscathed.

Rule #6: DON'T DO IT AND PRETEND YOU DID.

There are two categories to which this rule applies. In the first, the legislator takes credit for something he had absolutely nothing to do with. One former colleague used to issue a newsletter to all of his senior citizens immediately after Congress passed improved benefits in social security or medicare. Since many people confuse the roles of the state and federal governments, they are grateful to the first person who tells them about anything good any government does. So the colleague in question was beloved by his senior constituents. They, in turn, always loyally came through for him in some pretty tough elections, unaware that he actually did little or nothing for them.

In fact, newsletters can be the most effective method of continuing this tradition. One year when the legislature had to vote on whether to accept a pay increase, one Republican State Senator visited the House Republican caucus and lambasted members who were nervous about casting a positive vote. Not only was he adamant about demanding his salary increase, he insisted the House vote first. Since acceptance by one chamber automatically granted the raise to both, the second chamber was absolved from having to vote at all. Within days of his closed-door tirade, he sent out a newsletter to constituents damning the legislature's lust for more money and assuring his voters that he would oppose the increase. He got the raise, never had to vote on it, and all of his constituents gave him credit for voting against it. After all, that's what the newsletter said.

The second category of DON'T DO IT AND PRETEND YOU DID also takes advantage of the public's confusion about just how state government works. Many people, for example, believe that the introduction of a bill is tantamount to passage. Most legislators do get many of their best ideas from constituent suggestions, but some introduce a bill on every suggestion, request or gripe that comes in. This leads constituents to believe the legislator is really a good guy or, worse, that their perhaps unworkable, unrealistic and, in some cases, just plain idiotic idea is now law. The truth is that the legislators in question never even make any effort to have these bills taken up in committee. Why work on something that can't pass anyway when they've already received all the credit for accomplishing it?

Rule #7: NEVER MOVE WITHOUT AN ENTOURAGE.

Men seem to have a herd mentality. (See, also, Rule #10.) Perhaps this is a learned trait: they grew up in team sports.

In the legislature, this is translated into moving along with a pack of staff. Most male legislators seem unable to travel the hallways of the Capitol without a few "suits" following them. The number of "suits" multiplies with the prestige of the office: Brooks Brothers lives off the U.S. Senate. There's not only strength in numbers, there's prestige too. How could anyone know how important they are if several staff weren't clicking at their heels?

Women use staff differently than men. While our staff may well accompany us to some meetings, women tend to direct staff to do their research, to help prepare them for committee, to condense needed information which is then digested by the women legislators who present it alone to their colleagues. Consequently, they are often much better prepared than many of their male counterparts.

Men, on the other hand, wrap staff around themselves to produce an aura of importance. They use them as clones, seemingly unable to function without their mouthpieces. Not long ago, one such male legislator, in attempting to explain what he described as a rather complex bill to colleagues in committee, called upon his staff. The staff made the complex simple: the bill changed the number of people on a particular commission from three to five. Thank goodness for the "suits." How could the rest of us have read and understood the bill without them?

NEVER TRAVEL WITHOUT AN ENTOURAGE may explain why some staff feel justified in treating women legislators in the same sexist manner as their bosses do. They just get confused. They're all wearing the same suits.

Rule #8: THE POWER OF ONE

We hear it all the time: one person really can make a difference. A lot of people run for office on that theme. The men of the legislature believe it. At least when it comes to women. After all, what more do we need?

This rule has two uses. The first and most common is the doctrine that one woman anywhere is enough: on a committee, a commission, a board—in the legislature. If a second woman asks for a spot, she's often told, "We already have one, what more do you want?" Those of us who understand this rule know that it's very important when new committees or commissions are being drawn up in law to make sure the statutes explicitly require women. Further, since minorities are also often included, the statute must be written in such a way to exclude the possiblity of men's beloved "twofors," in which demands for both minorities and women result in one black woman. This practice is most visible when political parties, sensitive to balancing tickets, are picking slates at conventions. The ideal person to fill one slot would be a black Jewish woman of hispanic descent. Then the white men could keep everything else for themselves.

The second use of THE POWER OF ONE runs parallel to the first, but deals with issues. Should women succeed in enacting what men consider a "woman's issue," we become pests when we bring up another in the course of a decade: "Whaddaya mean we need this bill on children's nutrition? We just did one on breast cancer!" They have more important things to do.

Could it be we're pushing too hard? Naaaaah.

Could it be we expect too much? Naaaaah.

Could it be they fear we're taking over? Well, maybe.

Rule #9: WHENEVER NECESSARY, CHANGE THE RULES

Some time ago, I spoke to the President's Special Commission on Breast Cancer. My place on the agenda followed two male congressional staffers who both told of additional monies being directed to breast cancer in the coming budget. At the same time, they bemoaned the fact that huge Washington marches and vociferous lobbying by women were forcing their poor (male) bosses into what they referred to as "disease-specific" funding. They complained about the same problem being created by AIDS activists.

The truth is that health-related funding has always been disease-specific, specifically applying to white (straight) males. Once women figured that out and began demanding their fair share, the funding method suddenly had to become gender blind. In a way, it always had been. It was simply blind to women.

And in those critical, in-house legislative procedures, when women, by virtue of seniority, live long enough to be named committee chairs, it is not uncommon to see all the "important" bills (the ones the men are interested in) usually sent to that committee sent elsewhere. Or when women, by virtue of seniority and/or geography, ask for their rightful places on particular committees, they are told that they lack the appropriate "qualifications" or "experience." If we ask exactly what those newly created "qualifications" and "experience" entail, we are always given the same vague answer. Translation? We can't get it up.

It is, of course, pretty easy for our male colleagues to change the unwritten rules by which they live—indeed survive. It's not so easy to change the written ones. But when legislative leadership needs something done in a hurry, which usually means when they've been asleep at the switch for months or when a major holiday break is coming or when they're at risk of losing votes, it is not unheard of for them to break the written rules too, albeit apologetically.

Odd. These are the statutes that inevitably end up in court.

Breaking the unwritten rules never does. Nor are there ever any apologies.

Rule #10: STOP EVERYTHING! IT'S DEER HUNTING SEASON!

Having been a woman all my life, I was not particularly surprised by the first nine rules. But coming from a culture and a community where hunting plays no primal role, I must admit that I was completely taken aback my first November in the legislature when everything pretty much ground to a halt. It was the start of deer hunting season.

It doesn't matter what issues are before us, it doesn't matter if there's a crisis. When the Sacred Season starts, everything else stops.

In late 1993, we were in the middle of the state's most critical school funding crisis in its history. There was literally no money to open schools in the fall of 1994, and the end of 1993 was the practical deadline to resolve the problem. The Michigan Senate left for three weeks to go deer hunting.

While driving to Lansing for a special meeting on the issue during the Sacred Season, I heard a radio interview with one of our state senators explaining why it was really a good idea for the Senate to leave just as the school funding story was reaching its climax. I'd like to tell you what he said, but I was laughing so hard I missed most of it.

Actually, only a small minority of my colleagues are hunters, but for some reason we all have to pay homage to those who indulge in this most manly of manly tasks. I guess the rest of the men figure that even if they don't hunt, taking time off to honor the others puts them in the same league. They acquire, at least figuratively, the scent of their must.

I do not remember the press corps ever dwelling on or even mentioning the deer hunting breaks in the past, in spite of the fact that some colleagues accompany and are feted by lobbyists during their theoretical search for deer and their actual search for dough.

The mostly male press corps apparently can understand hunting season.

But a few years ago when women legislators
decided to use the days off to take a trip to Chicago
together, the press couldn't wait to find out what they
did, who paid for their meals, who arranged the trip.
It was in all the papers the next day.

One new woman colleague, so amused by the deer
tradition, decided to begin holding fundraisers during
deer hunting season. She is offering a free ticket to
people who drive up with a male colleague strapped
to the roof of the car, blood dripping from his mouth.

The event is open to the public. The male colleague
doesn't have to be from Michigan.

[7]

THE ROTARY

On east-coast highways, they have these things called rotaries. I hate them. Instead of just making a left turn like normal people do in the midwest, you get on a kind of circular cement island and keep driving around until you find the appropriate exit. The problem is that if you're not quite sure of your exit and if you're new to rotaries, you don't know where and how to get off. As you drive slowly in circles, everyone else is gesturing nastily at you for ruining their version of the Indianapolis 500. And you just keep rotating, your hands clutching the wheel, trying to get out.

Anyway, the other day while driving to the state capital, I had an epiphany. The legislature is like a rotary, only in this case, the problem is not getting out, but getting in. You can drive around in circles forever and never even find the entrance signs. If you're a woman. If you're a man, they always seem to be there; but if you're a woman, even if you're tailgating the male colleague in front of you, you can't find the signs. Ever.

The rotary is the nerve center of political power in both parties' caucuses. The people inside get to come out whenever they want to, but you can never follow them back in. And it is inside the rotary where all the deals are cut, where all the real decisions are made. When they meet in the men's room, it's called a redundancy.

Lest anyone not understand the rotary, lest newcomers or visitors to the legislature think that the fact of women's presence equates with women's input or power, they are subtly or not so subtly denied their illusions. For example, one of my male committee chairs recently introduced his otherwise all-male committee to the audience as Representative Jones, Representative Thomas, Representative Smith, and Maxine. Lobbyists, journalists and even male colleagues sometimes refer to women legislators by other women legislators' names. It's not just that "we all look alike," but that our names are not important enough to remember.

As women legislators gain in seniority, the rotary tightens even more. The problem is that the men in power sometimes can't deny women positions that are rightfully theirs, like committee chairs, so they simply shift the power someplace else...inside the rotary. For years, a woman chaired the House Labor Committee, but every time a major business-labor battle loomed, a group of men met somewhere else to negotiate the issues. The woman who chairs the House Insurance Committee, the acknowledged legislative expert on insurance law, found herself totally cut out of the process at the critical last moment of an insurance reform package. As long-time Chair of the House Elections Committee, I looked forward to running the legislative reapportionment process. After all, the man who had chaired that same committee ten years before did it. But when reapportionment time rolled around, I was told that a special, separate committee would be formed to handle redistricting, chaired by the same man who had run it ten years earlier. The mini bloodbath that ensued resulted in two separate, special committees. He chaired congressional redistricting; I chaired the state legislative process. Did that mean I won? Hardly. After ten months of my work, a group of powerful men got together on the last weekend before the maps were due and almost totally changed the agreed-upon configuration. I was told nothing about it until it was too late to do anything more than just protest. So even when you think you've finally gotten into the loop, they create another loop.

The existence of the rotary creates problems for more people than just women. Because the men of the rotary never really come out mentally, they remain totally cut off not simply from the reality of the legislative world, but the world in general. Consequently, brokered agreements between Republicans and Democrats, for example, are rarely related to the problem at hand, but, rather, to who can walk out of the rotary claiming more power. I suspect this is often measured in terms of inches.

This, in fact, is the real cause of gridlock, the etymology of which is probably "rotary" in Latin. Government does not come to a standstill because of mere partisan bickering or indecisive legislators or lobbyists and PACs. Government comes to a standstill because the most inner of the inner circle in both parties' rotaries spend most of their time attempting to cement their own power.

I'm not sure when all this began. Elements of it were probably always there, but things used to be different. There was a time when Republicans and Democrats all shared the same goals, but different ways of getting there. Not anymore. The only goal we share now is raw power and that can be achieved only by raw numbers.

Perhaps I shouldn't complain. If it weren't for the numbers game, women would never be supported by either party. Women candidates are sought out for one of two reasons: to run in hopelessly unwinnable seats so that the parties can pretend they promote women, or to run in close races that only a woman can win. In 1992, for example, I was frequently approached to run in a newly created congressional seat which was statistically solid Republican. I'm a Democrat. Frankly, I had little interest in Congress, but since no men of stature in my party even expressed a yawn over it, if I had aspired to greater heights, this was a real clue to my prospects for success. On the Republican side, meanwhile, high-powered men immediately began scrambling for position, and they were stunned, even angry, when a Republican woman had the unmitigated gall to enter *their* primary. These scenarios have been repeated numerous times across America's political landscape.

Women, therefore, become a valuable commodity in the legislative body count, unwitting tools in solidifying the power of a few men who spend much of their time trying to figure out how to block our pathways to the top. The only purpose of control is to keep control.

Every major vote is viewed as a way to win or lose majority status in a legislative chamber because whoever controls the majority also controls the process of redistricting when reapportionment comes around, even if it's ten years before the next census. Whoever controls redistricting controls the majority. (If this sounds like circular reasoning, don't forget we're talking about rotaries here.) So irresponsible bills and amendments are often introduced just to force the other side of the aisle into embarrassing votes. It doesn't really matter if anything passes as long as the rotary remains intact. Ergo, gridlock.

For example, in 1991, when Michigan's new Republican Governor decided to cut 183,000 people from General Assistance in order to balance the budget, the debate quickly shifted from the humanity of the decision to whether Democrats or Republicans would be more politically vulnerable in the process.

Most of the discussion in the generally disapproving Democratic caucus centered on whether we should all vote for the cut, thus ensuring passage, just to make the Governor and Republicans look bad and so use it against them in their reelection campaigns. Republicans, meanwhile, were already talking about campaign ads attacking Democrats for throwing more money down the "welfare sewer" while "good, solid working men and women *paid* for everything they got." Those legislators who kept bringing up the gruesome statistics of the people involved were looked upon by rotarians on both sides of the aisle as aliens from another world.

It's times like this when I seriously question whether getting into the rotary should be a goal. After all, do I really want to go through a door I may never be able to exit? And is the price paid for getting in really worth it?

Last year, one of my male colleagues was gallantly trying to teach me how to get invited to the yearly, all-expenses-paid conference at the posh Grand Hotel on Mackinac Island hosted by the Greater Detroit Chamber of Commerce. Somehow, my name has never shown up on the guest list.

My colleague thought he was helping me out. "See, Maxine, you have to show up at all their functions. Do you know you get points on how often you come? I just found that out last year." At this moment his voice became downright conspiratorial. "My wife and I make sure we attend everything. They actually grade you daily."

What he didn't understand was that I wasn't interested in going. He had mistaken the glazed look in my eyes for a lack of comprehension, rather than the stunned realization that one of my colleagues actually panders like this. I was trying hard not to throw up.

Around the same time, I discovered that some legislators were offered dirt-cheap rentals on state-owned vacation cottages on the same Mackinac Island. In this case, I didn't even know the practice existed, to say nothing of never having been offered a cottage. Nor was my name on the list of legislators mentioned in a newspaper article who were invited to spend spring break at a southern resort with a powerful lobbyist.

Whenever stories like this come out, my friends often call to tell me how glad they are that my name never appears. I'm grateful, too, of course, and want no part of it, but I don't think they understand all of the ramifications: only the rotary goes, often *en masse*.

This is why women are almost never connected with major political scandals. Of course, we're not born purists. Our names crop up in congressional check-writing violations and sometimes in bribes for votes. But when it comes to the mothers of all scandals, the real, sordid abuses of power, women's names aren't there. That's because we have no power to abuse.

Would it be different if we did? I'm not sure. Maybe not. Power can be pretty intoxicating. But the vast majority of women who run for office view power as a way to promote ideas, to effect change, not simply to accrue more power. And nothing is more frightening to the chief rotarians than legitimate ideas and change. When genuine debate on genuine issues becomes the standard procedure, instead of launching missiles toward the other side of the aisle, rotarians risk losing control. Nothing could be worse than a thinking legislature leading a thinking public.

So women and, yes, some men who'd like to see government offer proposals and move toward goals continue to drive around in circles. Our victories, if you can call them that, are often trimmed around the edges by power brokers who fear that good ideas might make good leaders—other good leaders.

It's a shame, really. Legislators perpetually doomed to be outsiders might actually strengthen the rotary if we were ever allowed into it. Blocked out forever, we have the potential to do some real damage. I think it was Lyndon Johnson who once said that it's better to have everyone inside the tent peeing out than to have one person outside the tent peeing in.

Like now.

[8]

PRO PRAYER, PRO FAMILY, PRO LIFE... PROPHYLACTICS

So the Prayer Lady came to visit me.

The Prayer Lady is a representative of the Michigan *Family* (emphasis theirs) Forum, one of Michigan's premier right wing groups. In a recent letter to legislators, the Forum expressed concern about the "growing desire of lawmakers for divine wisdom, compassion and courage to meet the demands of family and serving the public." They were jumping in to fill the heretofore unknown gap.

Not to worry, lawmakers. While the letter admitted the Forum was "unabashedly Christian," they absolutely promised that the prayer partners in our district, with whom they wished to personally connect us, would be absolutely nonsectarian and never, ever lobby us on any issues. On the other hand, legislators had to "respect those praying by not using the network for any purposes other than simply getting prayers answered."

I began praying for a trip to Hawaii.

The Prayer Lady, a human follow-up to the Michigan *Family* Forum letter, arrived in my office unannounced. She was not about to call in advance for an appointment and be rejected by 98 percent of the legislature.

She was gracious. I was gracious.

She had a smile frozen on her face. So did I.

She explained the program again.

I said, "I'm Jewish."

The corner of her smile twitched slightly. But she recovered. She mentioned a Rabbi she knew.

I said, "That's nice."

By that time, the five minutes she had requested were up. I told her that while I certainly had no problem with people praying for me, I wanted no part in the program, that I didn't believe it would be nonsectarian and certainly didn't believe it wouldn't be used for lobbying.

She left, still smiling.

A few weeks later, I received another letter from the Michigan *Family* Forum, telling me who my prayer partner was. They weren't giving up. Of course, the letter said, they would honor my request and my prayer partner would never call, but she would be praying for me throughout the year.

The line about "divine wisdom" *ad nauseum* "to meet the demands of family" *ad nauseum* was repeated at the end of the letter.

Actually, we spend a lot of time talking about family in the legislature. Well, actually, family *values*. Well, actually, arguing. The problem is that we can never agree on what family values are because we can never agree on what a family is.

The United States Census Bureau defines a family as "two or more persons, related through either birth, marriage or adoption, living under one roof". But in 1989, a national poll asked, "Which of the following comes closest to your definition of families?":

1. A group of people that is closely related by blood, marriage or adoption.

2. A group of people living in one household.

3. A group of people who love and care for each other.

4. I'm not sure about this.

Seventy-four percent chose number 3, twenty-two percent chose number 1.

The Michigan *Family* Forum and its legislative advocates would have undoubtedly chosen number 1. Thus, they would not recognize happy, well-adjusted children living with their unmarried parents as a family. Or happy, well-adjusted children living with gay parents. But unhappy, abused children living with their married parents are still a family.

In response to the plight of the latter, Michigan began a program called Families First within the Department of Social Services. The program's objective is to help troubled families stay together, rather than removing the children and placing them in foster care. While the program has some merit, it also has its disturbing elements.

For example, it did not originally occur to me that the primary reason for creating Families First was financial: it's a lot cheaper to keep all those unhappy campers together than it is to separate them. Nor had it ever occurred to me that the program would define incestuous families as those worthy to be "saved," a fact I discovered in a newspaper article about a dispute in my county's probate court involving just such a family.

I immediately proposed an amendment in the Appropriations Committee prohibiting the Department of Social Services from spending any funds to reunite families where incest had been a factor in the separation since none of us would be willing to place a child we loved in such a home. The amendment passed unanimously.

The short news story on the amendment prompted three interesting responses. First, I was visited by the Director of the Department of Social Services. He hoped I would agree to drop the idea. I wouldn't. He claimed my amendment might prevent the department from reuniting families where the perpetrator of the incest had been removed from the home, or that it would stymy efforts to help victims of incest by allowing judges and therapists to order counseling sessions in which the child is allowed to face her/his accuser. It didn't. But if that was all that was bothering him, I suggested he simply offer different wording. I also agreed to future committee discussions on the issue. Beyond that, I refused to budge.

The second response to my amendment occurred when the budget bill hit the floor of the House. One of my right wing colleagues, undoubtedly a Michigan *Family* Forum member, quietly and nervously approached me to ask if I intended to forge ahead. I did. He reminded me of my promise regarding committee hearings on the issue. I agreed again. His reluctance about my intervention in the Department's interventions was not a statement of support for incest, but a simple matter of fundamental religious/cultural belief: Save the family. At all costs. Except financial. As in poor families. And keep the legislature out of family business, which is loosely defined by the right wing as anything we do that they don't like.

The third and most interesting response to my amendment was from a woman representing a group known as C.U.R.E., who wished to meet with me. She supported the reunification of incestuous families. C.U.R.E. stands for Citizens United to Rehabilitate Errants. *Errants*? People who rape children are now called *errants*? What, I wondered, would this make an ax murderer?: A stumblebum?

I did not meet with the C.U.R.E.(d?) caller.

The legislature supported the budget with the amendment in it. A committee of the legislature has begun meeting on the issue. I can't wait to hear the testimony from the Michigan *Family* Forum.

Or the DADS Foundation, a first cousin to the Forum. Isn't that wonderful?: the moms do all the work and the DADS get the letterhead. (DADS, by the way, does not appear to be an acronym. It is just DADS.) Along with national groups like The Eagle Forum and Concerned Women for America, DADS also gets heavily involved in other family matters. Like family planning. They don't want any.

When we were named to co-chair the Appropriations Subcommittee on Public Health in 1993, my female Republican colleague and I succeeded in significantly increasing funds for family planning. While the budget bill specifically excluded abortion, it did include services for teenagers as well as adults.

When the Public Health budget came out of committee, I was approached by one of my far right wing colleagues who questioned me about the family planning money. I immediately assured him that abortion was not included, assuming that was his problem.

He: "Well, that's good. But...but...this language says we're going to do *outreach* too!"

I began to sense a larger problem looming on the horizon.

Me: "Right. In a lot of areas around the state, getting the word out is really hard."

He: "But...but...this includes *everybody*!"

Me: "You know, a lot of people who use these services are married."

I was trying desperately to be reassuring—not my

usual method of persuasion, but this money and this problem were far too important to risk an "in your face" fight.

A cloud began to descend upon him.

Me: "It's not a new program. Just expanding an existing one. We already do family planning."

More silence.

Then it hit me.

Me: "You *do* believe in contraception…don't you?"

He blanched. The cloud became a fog.

There would be trouble on the floor.

Almost every RWM (Right Wing Man) came armed with an amendment to the Public Health budget. Almost every PCW (Pro Choice Woman) was ready for them.

RWM: "I move to strike the entire section on family planning. This is just too much money. How can we afford it?"

Big mistake.

PCW: "We save anywhere from four to eighteen dollars for every dollar we spend on family planning. How can we not afford it?"

The amendment failed.

RWM: "I move to specify that family planning money can only be used to serve adults. We have to protect our children. This just encourages teenage sex."

The right wing has a tendency to refer to a cosmic "our children," though rarely in debates about poverty. In spite of their attempts to embrace the universal child, what they are apparently worried about is literally their own children. Since it is impossible to envision serious discussions about sexuality going on in their homes and since they believe that teenage sex would never happen if no one ever talked about it, spreading the information is the same as spreading a disease, one that *their* children just might catch.

PCW: "We have an epidemic of teenage pregnancies in this country. Have you forgotten what it was like to be sixteen in the back seat of a car?"

RWM: "I didn't own a car."

The amendment failed.

RWM: "I move to make family planning services available only to married couples."

PCW: "I'll support your amendment if you'll support mine mandating vasectomies for every boy in the state at age twelve, to be reversed when the young man turns eighteen."

The amendment failed.

RWM: "I move to limit family planning information to abstinence."

PCW: "If a fifteen year-old girl came to you and asked for information about birth control because she had made an irreversible decision to engage in
sex with her boyfriend, what would you tell her?"

RWM: "I'd tell her abstinence was the only way to guarantee she wouldn't become pregnant or contract a sexually transmitted disease."

PCW: "O.K., so you're right, but listen again. She's made up her mind. Let's assume you can't possibly change it. Without information and access to birth control, she may well become pregnant or diseased. What would you tell her then?"

RWM: "I'd tell her about abstinence. Period."

By the time he was through telling her, she'd be in her second trimester.

The amendment failed, but was supported by some men who've probably broken every moral code in the book. One of them was known to put his hands on everything in skirts he could find in every bar in Lansing, even after he became engaged, which is nowhere near as frightening as the fact that he will soon be spawning children.

The budget bill passed. But the debate, sure to continue, is typical: whenever the issue or even the word "family" comes up on the House floor, it is legislative DADS who jump up to sermonize. These are the men who quickly moved (unsuccessfully) to jail pregnant substance abusers for "delivering" drugs to a minor, but who opposed a crackdown on "deadbeat dads" for not delivering the money. They rail against programs for single welfare mothers as destroyers of families. They rail against spending money on the children of unwed mothers, having yet to make a connection between unplanned pregnancies and unplanned births. But they oppose family planning services for the same people because they don't want anyone outside the family planning it.

And who is left to fight them? The women of the legislature, representing the gender, married or single, that is still almost solely responsible for family care in

America. The thanks we get is to be labelled radical feminists and anti-family.

Almost inevitably, this particular battle of the sexes becomes a battle over sex. The main difference between right wing groups and progressive women legislators in this minefield is that the right wing basically views intercourse between unmarried people as immoral while we are more perplexed by the fact that young women are risking their health, their lives, and their futures if they engage in sex before they're ready or become teenage mothers. DADS are disgusted by the act itself, moms by the aftereffects. DADS view abstinence as the only answer; moms pose a lot more questions.

The truth is that virtually every woman legislator supports abstinence too. But those of us who also support providing information to teenagers about birth control are often accused of promoting promiscuous sex and opposing abstinence. That's simply not true. If I had my way, I would grab every underage young woman by her throat and strangle her until she cried "Abstinence!" Since that method is probably both impractical and illegal, it's necessary to turn to other procedures, like offering information to parents if they need help in speaking to their children about sex.

Undoubtedly the worst battle over family and, by extension, teenage sex, came during the lengthy and rabid debate over parental consent for abortion. During the committee hearing on the bill, Right to Life sent in a young woman in her twenties to support the bill. She told legislators she had always regretted not telling her parents about her teenage unplanned pregnancy and abortion. She also mentioned that when her younger sister became pregnant at sixteen (so much for teaching abstinence in their family), the younger daughter did tell their parents and was immediately thrown out of the house. (So much for teaching the importance of family in their family.)

Time after time in floor debates on parental consent, we were told by legislative DADS to keep our mitts off their families, that they and only they would make decisions about their children. No one else. Family rights must be preserved. But an interesting thing happened in a debate over "informed" consent for abortion, a bill designed to indoctrinate abortion-seeking women with right wing philosophy. Somehow, an amendment to exempt minors who had discussed the matter with their parents and had their parents' permission was soundly defeated. Family rights don't count when the right thinks they're wrong.

And when it came to debates over living wills and medical self-determination, our pro family colleagues opposed parents' rights to allow their daughter to die if an accident had left her in a persistent vegetative state. "Are you crazy?!" DADS yelled. "You can't trust the family. They might kill off a relative for a ten-cent life insurance policy!"

These "family battles" now even find their way into more mundane, less emotional issues—or at least what all of us thought were less emotional issues. For example, the right terms "Orwellian" state mandates requiring infant seats for toddlers and seat belts for older children. "We'll take care of our own families," they tell us. "Government has no compelling interest in our children." The reverse, of course, is true, when the "child" is a fetus. Then we are told of the state's compelling interest to protect it. The devil's in the definitions, as any good legislator can tell you.

Just as in the definition of "family" used by the Census Bureau and the right wing, who genuinely view blood, marital, or adoptive relationships as synonymous with loving relationships because they are absolutely blind to any households that aren't identical to theirs. Unfortunately, they're wrong.

During the year-long battle over parental consent, for example, many newspaper stories attested to the Census Bureau's fractured definition of family: the father who poured flammable liquid on his pregnant teenage daughter and set her on fire; the drug-addicted mother who allowed her crack-happy, alcoholic, live-in boyfriend to sleep with her thirteen-year-old daughter whenever he wished, ultimately impregnating her; the twelve-year-old boy who went to court to terminate his parents' rights, a termination that his father wasn't even interested in opposing; and case after case of children being battered and/or murdered by their parents. And these are just the stories we find out about. All promotions for a Families First policy? Or all indictments of it?

It's a tough call.

So we continue to fight, although on a pretty slippery slope. It's very difficult to argue with people who want nothing to do with sex yet see it everywhere. Who oppose government intervention except when they demand it. Who spread their arms with love to encompass everyone, unless the everyone doesn't look or behave as they do.

This, of course, includes the "look" of the women of the legislature. Simply by virtue of our elections if nothing else, we don't quite mesh with the right wing's ideal definition of liberated women, explained by Beverly LaHaye, president of Concerned Women for America: "Spirit-controlled women are truly liberated because they are totally submissive to their husbands."

"Spirit-controlled?" Me? You mean there's still hope?

Perhaps that's why they and my prayer partner keep praying for me.

Probably to burn in Hell.

[9]

THE FETUS, THE FORMER WOMEN, THE FLYING NUN AND ME

Life in the Trenches of the Abortion Battle

My favorite group is back in Lansing: Former Women of Choice. They're pretty easy to spot because they roam the halls of the Capitol carrying large placards or wearing sign boards with their name on it.

The arrival of the Former Women is a sure sign that another abortion vote is about to take place. Before they first appeared about two years ago, we had to take our cue from the ubiquitous Right to Life lobbyist slithering around the hallways. He's pretty tiny, though very fertile as he once told me, and so a little harder to find. Besides, he doesn't spend a lot of time hanging around my office.

I lead the pro choice forces in the Michigan House of Representatives. Though I've probably read millions of words about abortion, none really describe how the abortion legislation process unfolds in the legislature. Newspaper headlines scream vote totals, but few people know the behind-the-scenes work, the strategy, and, yes, sometimes the machinations that lead up to those totals. From my perspective, it's a far more interesting story.

The early 1980s were the days when the only choice debate in Michigan was whether we would continue to pay medicaid funds for poor women who sought abortions. We were one of only fourteen states, along with the District of Columbia, which still did, "proving," according to Right to Life, our status as a true anomaly. What they neglected to mention was that the fourteen states and Washington D.C. accounted for almost 40 percent of the United States population. Further, seven other states allowed for several exemptions to their medicaid bans over and above saving the life of the mother: rape and incest, mental health, fetal abnormality, none of which were to be allowed in Michigan. If the populations of those seven states were added to our fourteen, the total was 53 percent of the nation.

But providing statistics or logic in this debate is generally worthless. Anti abortion organizations habitually disseminate outrageous facts and figures. By the time we track down the reality, their "truth" has already sunk in. For example, a few years ago every legislator received a newsletter from the Christian Media Exchange which referenced a study "proving" that saline abortion is second only to heart transplants as the elective surgery with the highest fatality rate in the United States. I knew it wasn't true, if for no other reason than that saline abortions are extraordinarily uncommon, so I wrote to the Christian Media Exchange and asked for a copy of the study. Naturally, it was based on another "study" which took several months to track down. The originating study turned out to be an anti abortion tract written before *Roe* when illegal, botched abortions did kill many women and when heart transplants were so rare and unsophisticated that some of the donors were almost outliving the recipients.

Even more insidious, last year one of my anti abortion colleagues distributed page 29 from a national Planned Parenthood document which cited the Alan Guttmacher Institute in agreement with anti choice studies "proving" that 91 percent of women who have abortions suffer post-procedural trauma. (They *love* to cite Guttmacher, Planned Parenthood's main research source.) It was false. An anti abortion group had gotten hold of the Planned Parenthood document, created a new page 29 which looked identical to all the other pages, and distributed the whole throughout the country.

But the abortion battle was still a little simpler twelve years ago when the new Democratic Governor, James Blanchard, stood squarely for abortion rights as did his Republican predecessor, William Milliken, for fourteen years before that. Both of them consistently vetoed line items in the social services budget outlawing medicaid payments for abortions. The anti choice forces always had, and still have, a majority in the legislature, but they lacked the two-thirds vote necessary to override a gubernatorial veto. So every year the legislature voted to ban medicaid abortion funding and every year the Governor vetoed it and every year the veto was upheld and every year we paid.

Medicaid funding should be a simple issue of equity. As long as abortion remains legal, poor women deserve the same access to health care that everyone else does. But the central theme for those in the choice movement should never waver from choice itself, since all of the sidebars—medicaid funding, parental consent, "informed" consent, *ad nauseum*—are simply tools to eliminate access and where there is no access, there is no choice. No one knows this better than anti choice organizations which have deftly succeeded in distracting the generally pro choice public from their real purpose of eliminating abortion altogether.

Right to Life opposed medicaid funding because it meant their tax dollars were being spent on something which they consider immoral. Whose aren't? Using their Polling Company from Hell, they flooded us with statistics "proving" not only their moral superiority, but their statistical superiority as well. It wasn't necessarily that I doubted their numbers; it was just that I suspected that the real opinion of most people polled was anti welfare, which often translates into anti black.

My active involvement in legislative abortion battles actually began in the second year of my first term. I decided to sit in on a committee meeting to review the budget for Michigan's protective services agency which oversees abused and neglected children. Michigan was still recovering from a severe economic depression during which our entire budget had been cut by almost one third. Social services took the biggest hit and nowhere was the disaster more agonizing than in protective services. Workers' caseloads had grown to thirty or forty families a month. About all they could do was to check periodically to make sure the kids in their charge were still living. Sometimes, they weren't.

The committee hearing was not filled with bleeding heart liberals, but with police officers and sheriffs and prosecutors, many of them huge, muscular men, who were quite literally begging us, some of them in tears, to increase the budget. They passed out pictures of beaten, often dead children. We only had to look at the pictures. They had to deal with the reality. The problem was getting worse. They simply couldn't stand it anymore.

After two hours of some of the most grotesque, nauseating testimony I've heard in my six terms in the legislature, I returned to my office and found a small, hand-wrapped box of candy, a gift from Right to Life of Michigan. It was Valentine's Day, 1984. The card said something about saving unborn children. I was furious. It must have taken hours to hand-wrap 148 boxes and it took hours that morning for Right to Life supporters to distribute them in legislative offices. But not one of those people or their paid staff or lobbyist came to that hearing on protective services. The die was cast. I was in it for the long haul.

Election Day, 1984, proved as revolting as Valentine's Day had been. The Reagan landslide swept many legislative Democrats from office, a number of whom were pro choice. When the dust cleared, we found ourselves four votes short of being able to sustain a gubernatorial veto. But Governor Blanchard was adamant. He was not going to be overridden. I don't know if the issue was choice or the embarrassment of any override, but in this business, you learn to use any crumb that's thrown your way.

I was asked to attend the first strategy session shortly after the election. I was stunned. The general discussion revolved around who we could "turn" with gubernatorial favors. "Are you crazy?" I yelled at them. "Right to Life supporters are in legislative districts right now, picketing legislative homes, making vicious phone calls, harassing legislators' families. And we're talking about building a road in someone's district to win a vote? If they're threatening, we should threaten too." My Republican colleague, Shirley Johnson, agreed with me, but our lobbying support groups, the pro choice organizations, were pretty feeble then. They could round up some letters and phone calls to legislative offices, but they were no match for the size and coordination of the Right to Life lobby.

As in most states, when *Roe* was decided in 1973, Michigan's pro choice groups just patted themselves on the back and went home. It was a deadly mistake.

Right to Life immediately began organizing grass roots supporters and were so far ahead of us that it would take years to catch up.

Few other organizations can strike fear in the hearts of elected officials like Right to Life does. Their methods aren't pretty; persuasion is not their long suit. They simply threaten political death. In fact, they have now become so brazen that instead of sitting in the audience during committee hearings on bills in which they have an interest, their lobbyist sometimes stands right next to the committee table giving signals and directions on every issue and amendment that comes up. It wouldn't surprise me if they demanded a seat on the House floor next.

Having spoken to many colleagues who vote with them, it is clear that only about one-third genuinely oppose abortion. Another third is clearly pro choice, but terrified of Right to Life. The rest really care little about the issue and simply see the anti choice side as the most politically expedient. Of course, almost all of these people are men, so it doesn't affect them anyway.

Undaunted by these fears and attitudes, our post-election strategy group began a systematic review of Right to Life's legislators, came up with seven or eight potential vote switchers and commissioned polls in four of their districts. The results were amazing. Their constituents were solidly pro choice and ran about 50/50 on medicaid funding. Not amazing, when voters who opposed medicaid funding were asked if they were willing to support increasing the social services budget to pay for the additional babies that would undoubtedly be born to poor women, 35-40 percent said "No." Perhaps most beneficial to our cause was the question asking voters if they knew how their own legislator voted on the issue of medicaid funding. Eighty percent or more didn't have a clue, and of the 20 percent who answered, about half were wrong. We met with the legislators involved. Two swung our way.

And then there was Ethel Terrell, or E.T., as she was affectionately known. Suffice it to say that describing Ethel as being out in left field was to give her credit for being in the ball park. She was an older black woman who simply had a difficult time relating to the legislative process.

Ethel was an outspoken opponent of abortion, one of only three in the sixteen member legislative black caucus. Fortunately, she was also pretty amenable to gubernatorial attention, but the problem was that no one knew what she wanted, and if anything had been offered, she was shrewd enough to up the ante. So we left her in the hands of other black caucus members who worked her mercilessly.

Ultimately, on the day of the budget vote itself, not the override, we played our best card. We invited a very powerful black minister to give the invocation. He had had many "chats" with Ethel about her vote on this issue and she was terrified of him. When the votes were cast, she was with us, a black caucus member and the minister standing near her to make sure she did the right thing.

But the critical vote was the coming override. Our two crossovers were holding, but that still left us two short. It should have only been one, but we could never be sure of Ethel, who checked herself into a hospital about a month before the vote. Right to Life types visited and sent flowers, priests and ministers. So did we. She enjoyed the attention so much that every now and then she forgot to be terrified of the upcoming vote. But then the press caught on. Ethel checked herself out of the hospital. No one knew where she was.

The day of the override vote was excruciating. My colleague, Shirley Johnson, and I spent the morning nervously calling and visiting the Governor's chief aide on the project, who repeatedly assured us that we had the votes. The fourth had finally come our way after some truly inspirational lobbying by the pro choice groups and the promise of a long-sought favor from the Governor.

Shirley and I drank our lunch. It had no effect; adrenaline conquers all. But our fears were not without reason. As with any major issue, especially an emotional one, votes simply can't be counted until they're cast.

Adding to our anxiety was the presence of a huge Right to Life contingent who had flocked to the state capital to finally savor the victory they had waited for for over sixteen years. So sure were they of their success that they had already introduced their next piece of legislation, a bill to outlaw all abortions for all public servants. It was probably a tactical mistake. For years we had pointed out that taxpayer dollars were paying for abortions through public employee insurance packages and that Right to Life was attacking only the poor because they were the most vulnerable. The introduction of the employee bill after sixteen years didn't get them off the hook. Rather, it served to justify our warning that after the poor, everyone else would follow, an accusation Right to Life had consistently denied.

It was amusing watching anti choice Democrats cringe when they suddenly realized they'd have to choose between caving in to Right to Life or caving in to the labor unions. As one of them told me, "We can't do this. This is a *contractual* issue. I mean, this includes *everybody.*" So much for strong beliefs. Once, on the floor, I even offered anti choice legislators a chance to sign a form asking that abortion coverage be omitted from their personal policies. No one took me up on it. Apparently, some of them had daughters. In over ten years of battles on the abortion issue, that bill has never been introduced again.

But Right to Life was still laughing that fateful morning, especially whenever they saw us. And we couldn't help but wonder if our four supposed switches might not be matched by four of theirs that we didn't know about, since only one of ours had made his new position public.

Right to Life stopped laughing and I started about 2:30 p.m. when the vote was taken. Our votes held. The Governor's veto was sustained. Chaos broke out on the floor. The press went berserk. Session was immediately adjourned. And I couldn't stop laughing, mostly, I think, in relief, but also because at least three reporters rushed up to me demanding to know where the absent Ethel Terrell was. They insisted I knew. Me? One accused me of hiding her in my basement. I don't have a basement.

That day was a landmark in Michigan legislative abortion battles. For the first time, Right to Life had suffered a major, unexpected blow and the papers couldn't stop talking about it. For the first time, pro choice groups and legislators were not looked upon as a bunch of ineffectual wimps. For the first time, it was pro choice *women* legislators that the press flocked to for quotes.

For all my concerns about elected men ignoring issues specifically affecting women, I strongly believe that choice is a debate which should be carried by women. After all, it's our bodies and futures at stake. While there are many wonderful pro choice male legislators, it's still much harder for an anti abortion legislator to look me in the eye on this vote than at a man. At that point, it simply becomes another old-boys' ball game. Over the years, we have learned when to highlight our male friends, when to let them carry the ball, but the debate is and always will be about us.

Months before the override vote, Shirley and I decided to wrest control of the issue from pro choice male colleagues. Wonderful as these men had been for so many years defending the issue, they were simply

unwilling to break away from the gentlemanly rules-of-
the-game way of handling the matter. Consequently,
their voices were simply never heard in the media.
Only Right to Life was quoted because their words
were so much more volatile, so much better copy.
They were the only ones quoted when they won the
budget votes. They were the only ones quoted when
they lost the overrides. That had to stop. Shirley and I
agreed that even though we lacked the organizations
behind us, we were every bit as capable of verbal
flame throwing as they were. Changing the terms and
the tone of the debate was a conscious, carefully
thought-out decision.

So flame throwing we did and flame throwing we
continue to do. And now we are quoted. It is true that
some newspapers have criticized us for the heat of our
words, a criticism never leveled at Right to Life, but
they do quote us. For me, it's really quite cathartic.
Also fun.

For pro choice organizations, it's critical. Anti
abortion groups, for example, have a charming tendency to mail out bottles containing dead fetuses. We,
on the other hand, never show our pre-*Roe* pho-
tographs of women lying dead in deserted rooms, victims of botched abortions. Nor should we, necessarily.
But moderate voices win no fights against religious
zealotry and abortion is, first and foremost, a religious
issue. We won nothing with genteel arguments of
equity, the theme our male pro choice colleagues had
used for years. So we switched the argument to

choice, pure and simple. Then we zeroed in on issues like rape and incest, using them every chance we got, our drumbeat, as it were.

Right to Life of Michigan refused to allow exceptions in the medicaid ban for rape and incest because their position is that a fetus is a life is a fetus, no matter what the circumstances of conception. While they may deserve some points for consistency, few arguments more compellingly reveal their willingness to subvert the constitutional rights and well-being of a woman to the supposed constitutional rights of a fetus. In the face of that accusation, which they hate, they have a standard answer: "It never happens anyway. No one becomes pregnant as a result of rape." No one? Pressed further, they present new "studies" (I swear they carry hundreds of them on every topic everywhere they go) showing that only 1 percent of rapes result in pregnancy. And after all, why even have a debate over 1 percent?

Figures in other studies not commissioned by Right to Life estimate the pregnancy rate resulting from rape at at least 4-7 percent and incest-related pregnancy figures are far higher because of the repetitiveness of the crime. But let's use Right to Life's figures. In 1992, there were approximately 7500 *reported* rapes in Michigan and, according to FBI statistics, only about 1 in 10 rapes is ever reported. Also, about half of all rape victims are under twenty. So using FBI estimates and Right to Life's 1 percent solution, of the potentially 75,000 Michigan rapes in 1992, about 750 women were impregnated, half of whom were under twenty. But since it never happens anyway, why get excited? As one of my male anti choice colleagues once explained, sperm reacts differently during a rape.

And you think this issue can't be fun?

Fun never lasts long in the legislature, though. Right to Life just doesn't take kindly to embarrassing defeats. The following year, 1986, was the most vicious. There was a terrible struggle between the House and Senate over decisions on the social services budget, which had nothing to do, initially, with abortion. It's always a tough budget to pass because the poor aren't particularly popular in the legislature. The battle lasted through October 1, the beginning of our fiscal year. A three-month extension budget was passed, but as the new deadline approached, there was only minimal progress in the dispute between the two legislative chambers.

After the legislature adjourned for the winter holidays with an agreement on another three-month extension, Right to Life dropped the ultimate bombshell: their state senators, who controlled the budget in that body and pretty much of everything else, reversed themselves and said there would be no extension, that all social services payments would end on January 1 if Michigan continued to pay for abortions. Their gloves were off. The Governor cannot veto a budget that does not exist.

It's one of the dirtiest things I've seen in eleven years. I took my gloves off too. So did a lot of others.

Even many anti choice legislators were stunned. The poor had nothing to do with this fight. Right to Life and their legislative lackies were far beyond threatening poor pregnant women. They were now threatening the over 65 percent of nursing home patients on medicaid. They were now threatening Children's Hospital of Michigan, over 60 percent medicaid funded, along with many other major hospitals in the state. And they were threatening prenatal care for poor women who *wanted* to have their babies and the health and well-being of all their children.

Right to Life defended itself vigorously against the assault from pro choice legislators. (In fact, if the situation hadn't been so dire, we probably would have been downright gleeful for the opening.) It was not their fault, but ours. If we really cared about the poor, we could simply give up abortion. But the media and the general public never bought their arguments. The blame was clearly on them.

Even the Catholic Church, which had played along with all the other obnoxious little games over the years, backed away. And the Church was even more embarrassed when a short, squat little nun suddenly appeared in the Capitol, making unannounced visits to the offices of anti choice House members. She threatened them with hell and damnation if they did not go along with Right to Life. No one ever knew where she came from, including the Catholic Church, and, when the issue was resolved, no one ever knew where she went. Right to Life claimed they knew nothing about her, but how else could she have known so quickly about the vote? And who paid for her air travel? She said she was from Texas and traveled the country on a mission to save the unborn. We called her The Flying Nun. She was a truly nasty little woman, but probably provided the pro choice side with our only bit of levity during the entire, awful episode.

The legislature was called back for an emergency session, by which time Shirley and I were really flexing our muscles. Since this entire incident took place shortly after an American plane had been hijacked in the Middle East and we had all seen pictures of the hijackers throwing dead hostages from the plane, I couldn't resist the analogy. I stood on the floor and accused Right to Life of being no better, of holding the poor and infirm hostage for their own narrow ideological purposes, of throwing children, one by one, from the roof of Children's Hospital. Shirley began singling out anti choice legislators by name, ripping into them mercilessly. She was gaveled down. Apparently, while it is not considered gentlemanly to personally attack a colleague on the floor, it is considered gentlemanly to kill off the entire social services budget.

Fortunately, Right to Life lost again that day. While they won easily in the Senate, fourteen members of the overwhelming anti choice majority in the House put their collective foot down and voted against the bill. They deserve a lot of credit. In fact, one of the few things that has ever worked in our favor over the years is Right to Life's willingness to go beyond any

bounds of tactical decency for their cause, to be decid-
edly unchristian for the sake of being good Christians.

With two resounding defeats in two years, the mis-
sionaries to the unborn were not a happy bunch.
Armed with a new, more reactionary group of legislative leaders, they finally fell upon the fail-safe solution: a citizen initiative. Michigan's Constitution
allows citizens to present the legislature with petitions
to enact laws. Like any other bills, the initiatives need
only a simple majority vote; but unlike other bills,
they cannot be vetoed by the Governor. They are very
rarely used, mostly because they require about
250,000 signatures, far too burdensome for the vast
majority of organizations. But not for Right to Life,
which is extraordinarily well-funded, well-organized,
and well-disciplined. Plus, as one of my pro choice
colleagues pointed out, "This will take them about
two Sundays in church." In fact, they didn't need
much more.

There was no suspense on the day of the vote. This
one wasn't fun. Right to Life's lock-step majority came
through.

After an obligatory press conference following our
defeat, I left the legislature, left the capital, and drove
home. It was a seventy-five mile drive through tears. I
don't cry easily and the grief had less to do with losing than with the feeling that I had just let down hundreds of thousands of Michigan women. Those of us
who become deeply involved with issues like this
become deeply attached to the people supporting our

position and they to us. They depend on our judgment, our advice, our political savvy. When we win, we win for everyone. When we lose, we lose for everyone too.

Not that it was over. The pro choice organizations immediately began a petition drive to place the newly passed law on the 1988 ballot as a referendum. Other states had been successful. Why not us? Easy. We weren't organized.

The referendum election, following a bumbling but ultimately successful-because-we-paid-for-signatures petition drive, would coincide with the Dukakis/Bush election in November. The hardest decision to make was whether to use the money issue. For all my years of involvement and all the years before that, we had never, ever played that game. While Right to Life continually screamed out that Michigan was spending $7 million a year on what they often referred to as 19,000 "welfare abortions," we never made the counter argument that not paying for abortions would ultimately cost the state millions more in prenatal care, birth, postnatal care, and general care and feeding of another ADC child. It is grotesque reasoning. Poor women who want to have children should be allowed to have them and the government should help with their care. Money should not be the issue. Actually, this is one point on which Right to Life and I agree. But their concerns for the poor ring hollow. Their attempt to kill off the entire social services budget is only one example of that.

But this was war and we uncomfortably played

the money card, as well as almost any other we could think of. In ad after ad, Right to Life assured Michigan voters that other states that had ceased funding medicaid abortions had experienced no increase in children born to women in poverty. They pointed to an article in the *Wall Street Journal* for support, an article that, once again, made its point by distorting information from the Alan Guttmacher Institute. We produced statistics that they were lying. No one believed us.

Their ads were slick and incessant. Ours were O.K. and sporadic. The pro choice groups were simply unable to raise the necessary money. I even went to the fundraisers for the Dukakis campaign, with which I was heavily involved, to ask for help. I told them that like it or not, their fate was inextricably tied to ours. They didn't believe me. Dukakis lost Michigan by more than 2-1. So did we.

Postscript:

Of course, we went to court. About two months after the ban took effect, an impoverished minor, impregnated by rape, sued the state with the ACLU as her attorneys. The pro choice side ultimately lost in the Michigan Supreme Court.

About two years after the ban, the Department of Social Services released figures showing a significant increase in births to poor women. Right to Life said they didn't think there was any connection and, besides, they had never claimed there wouldn't be more births.

[10]

"GIVE A WOMAN A FISH AND SHE'LL EAT FOR ONE DAY. TEACH A WOMAN TO FISH AND SHE'LL BEAT YOU IN THE NEXT ELECTION"

—EMILIO's List

During the recent architectural restoration of the Michigan Capitol to its original 1870s glory, workers found several interesting items as they tore out walls and punched out ceilings. One such curiosity was a box of papers from a long-departed legislator, EMILIO (Elected Men Insist Liberation Is Out) Everyman. Senator Everyman led the state's legislative battle against the Nineteenth Amendment, farsighted enough to understand that once men let women have the right to vote, they might just want to hold office too. In his list of thoughts on the matter, EMILIO was clearly far ahead of his time. Almost all of his political descendants have now caught up with him.

O.K., so we did it. We pulled off The Year of the Woman. The 1992 Year of the Woman followed about twelve failed attempts in the twelve years before that. And what were the major hallmarks of The Year of the Woman?: Adding four and eventually five new women to the *U.S.* (Uno Sex) Senate, for a grand total of 7 percent, and 23 new women to the *U.S.* (Uno Sex) House, for a grand total of 10.8 percent.

Most women call that progress. Most elected men and the thousands if not millions of male wannabes who threw their diapers into the ring shortly after they left the womb call it an infestation, a deadly, unstoppable infection. Something like political AIDS. To political men, women have become the unsafe sex.

"Familiarity breeds condescension"
—*EMILIO's List*

In America, once a disease has been discovered, work begins on a cure. So forming something akin to the political Center for Disease Control, our male colleagues began an intensive research program. They quickly figured out that women were the sole carriers of the disease but never caught it. Only men caught it. And only men died. They called the disease Typhoid Emily.

Women called it *EMILY's List*.

EMILY (Early Money is Like Yeast) began in 1985 for the specific purpose of increasing the number of Democratic women in Congress and statewide office. $100 buys a membership and a commitment to give at least $100 each to two of *EMILY's* endorsed candidates nationwide. In its first few years of existence, *EMILY's List* was moderately successful, basically attracting politically aware women who were probably already giving money. Even after *EMILY's* significant contributions to the 1990 victory of Texas Governor Ann Richards, few political men paid attention. They just thought it was cute. How were they to know it was the bad seed?

> "Women in politics makes bedfellows strange."
> —*EMILIO's List*

Then Anita Hill happened and millions of pissed-off women began looking for revenge. Many of them found it in women's political PACs, particularly *EMILY's List*, clearly the most sophisticated of the groups.

In 1992, *EMILY's List* was the most successful fundraising organization in the country, collecting over $6 million for its endorsed candidates. There is no question that it was a major factor in electing all four new Democratic women in the *U.S.* Senate and nineteen of the twenty-one new Democratic women in the *U.S.* House.

EMILY's success was not only at the ballot box but in spawning imitators, like the Republican *WISH* (Women in the Senate and House) *List*. While these two organizations support only pro choice women, early in 1993, anti choice women began forming similar groups. Talk about a fast-spreading disease.

"These are the times that try men's polls."
—*EMILIO's List*

It had to stop...men said. And quicker than you can say "erection," bundling, the practice of collecting many checks and turning them over at once to a candidate (*EMILY's* stock-in-trade), became a scourge that simply had to be erased from the political landscape.

Bundling is about as old as Congress is, not to mention many of its male members. While in a very general sense, it is what every fundraiser does, in a more specific sense, bundling is the practice of multi-client lobbyists collecting PAC checks from several clients and delivering them to candidates in a "bundle." Thus, even when a multi-client lobbyist speaks to an officeholder on behalf of a single client, the lobbyist represents many clients—and thousands of dollars in PAC checks—at once, and the elected official knows it.

"PAC up your troubles. Come on, get happy."
—*EMILIO's List*

Funny. In all its years of failed efforts at campaign finance reform, Congress has never before shown much concern about bundling. But when over 4 percent of your members are killed off in one year, the only way to protect your own member is through drastic action. In its only act of genuine, warm bipartisanship in 1993 and its first agreement in nineteen years on campaign finance reform, the *U.S.* Congress moved to outlaw bundling. Look, fighting a disease is like fighting a *WAR* (Women Against Rules). And as everyone knows, we always come together in *WAR*time.

> "There are no foxes in a foxhole."
> —*EMILIO's List*

The truth is that *EMILY's* List bundling is not really analogous to multi-client lobbyist bundling. Most important, *EMILY* does not lobby. Further, while lobbyists bundle huge PAC checks to empower themselves, *EMILY* bundles thousands of small checks from individuals to empower the candidates it supports. And that's exactly what the problem is for the ocean of men that is Washington. Bundling is supposed to empower lobbyists who in turn empower officeholders (read "men"), not the people who run against them (read "women"). Women had finally figured out the trick, but they were using it for the *wrong purpose*. Under the Geneva conventions, this is a legitimate reason to initiate hostilities.

It stands to reason that if the *FOE* (Fear of *EMILY*) was rampant in Washington, it would seep down to the states. In Michigan, it didn't take long for male legislators to see their manifest destiny to higher office withering away.

So the 92 percent male Michigan Senate, led by a

very male, very Republican *GOV* (Guys Only Vicinity) voted to prohibit out-of-state money from being matched by state funds in Michigan's publicly funded gubernatorial campaign. And none of this, trust them, had anything to do with the fact that a Democratic woman was running for *GOV* in 1994, certain to be a recipient of *EMILY's* largesse. Nope, totally unrelated, the *DOOFUSES* (Defenders Of Our Faith) told us: it's just sinful to use state taxpayers' dollars to match contributions from outside the state. Apparently, this was not sinful in 1990 when the current male *GOV* did it approximately two hundred times.

> "You gotta know when to hold 'em,
> know when to scold 'em."
> —*EMILIO's List*

But wait. This only applies to the *GOV*. What about all those women (19.5 percent) currently overrunning the legislature who might just run against their male colleagues in future congressional races? Gripped by the *FOE* as well, the Michigan State Chamber of Co*MM*erce (the two M's in Co*MM*erce stand for misogyny twice over) sent an *SOS* (Save Our Sex) to the SOS (Secretary of State), asking him to declare *EMILY* a political committee according to Michigan law. That meant *EMILY* could bundle no more than $500 worth of checks per candidate, rather than the thousands per candidate it now often distributes. Talk about covering all the bases.

Those of you whose eyebrows are arched about as high as they can go and whose eyeballs have rolled so far back in your head that you can actually see your brain must understand that there was not an iota's worth of sexism in any of this. This is because the Michigan Senate managed to get their only female Republican member to sponsor the bill.

It was not surprising to see the Phyllis Schlafly Syndrome visiting the Michigan Senate, which is only just now beginning to inch its way into the 17th Century. In a cross between political peek-a-boo and the emperor's new clothes, senators figured if they could just find one skirt to hide behind, no one could see the rest of them.

And why did the skirt do it? While she would undoubtedly seek a patent for the idea, it's doubtful if she was the inventor. Perhaps as an anti choice woman with aspirations for higher office herself, the state senate sponsor feared going up against a competitor from *WISH* or *EMILY* in the future. In addition, the power and persuasion of the *GOV's* office is incredible. It's pretty hard to say "No" when the big man comes calling.

In the House, the bill went to a 93 percent male committee. (Of course, which aren't?) It is interesting to note that some years earlier, the then Speaker of the House moved all campaign finance bills from the Elections Committee to the House Oversight Committee. That's because the new Chair of the House Elections Committee was a woman: me. It wasn't personal. It was pure gender. Since money is the most treasured of the men's treasure chests, allowing a woman to determine how it can be distributed might well lead to disaster, not to mention more women in office. Synonyms, actually.

During the House hearing, only one of the men suggested to the senate sponsor that her bill was the most callously hypocritical and transparent he had ever seen. Considering how many callously hypocritical and transparent pieces of legislation we pass, that's really saying a lot.

"Omnia genitalis vincit."
—EMILIO's List

Much of the rest of the committee wore its good government face, the special one that men put aside and only use when they're about to enact bad government. It is a somber, yet somehow warm face, brows slightly furrowed, eyes intensely interested, lips pursed slightly, ready to speak in a voice that is about an octave lower than usual. The total demeanor includes a military posture, shoulders back, tie straight, jacket buttoned, fly zipped. (If the fly's unzipped, it can pretty much ruin the whole picture.) They always cross their fingers that the press won't figure it out. The press never does.

In fact, a number of newspaper editorials supported the so-called reforms regarding *EMILY's List* and bundling in the Michigan legislature and *U.S.* Congress. Most papers are so anxious for campaign finance reform that they'll take just about anything and it's so easy for them to identify with elected officials since 90 percent of the nation's editors are men too. One such editorial patronizingly assured women that eliminating practices like bundling would *ultimately* lead to more women in office because it would level the playing field. That's what they said about the last major campaign finance reforms in 1974, which immediately lowered the number of women in Congress. The problem is that a level playing field has little value if you're not allowed on the field in the first place. And "ultimately" could well mean three hundred years.

> "If it's good for *GM* (Government Men),
> it's good for the country."
> —*EMILIO's List*

There were too many women attending the House hearing on the bill for the sponsor or committee members to drag out the *"EMILY's List* is a Special Interest" line. That accusation began to wear pretty thin after the first woman asked how 51 percent of the population could be considered a special interest. So the committee members, ever smiling down upon the women testifying against the bill, explained that it was their solemn duty to protect unwitting taxpayers from having their voluntary contributions to our public gubernatorial campaign fund match sinful out-of-state money. I asked, "Why not just give citizens that information on their tax forms and let them make the decision?" No one answered. Perhaps they're still researching it.

My good Democratic colleagues on the committee had a real problem. They didn't want to do anything to help the Republican *GOV*, but they didn't want to miss out on being part of the team that would eradicate Typhoid Emily. Who knows who they might have to run against next? So when it came time for the *VOTE* (Vigorous Opposition To Equality), the committee approved the bill but highmindedly moved its effective date to 1995. They would wait until the 1998 gubernatorial campaign to decimate women.

> "'We hold these truths to be self-evident;
> that all men are created equal....' Period."
> —*EMILIO's List*

In a political situation like this, there are two options: one is to deny colleagues an amendment they really want; the other is to force them to support an amendment they really don't want. If the latter amendment is successful, it will effectively kill the bill. In order to save *EMILY*, we managed to find both.

During the course of the day when the bill was to be taken up on the 75 percent male House floor, I was approached by representatives from the *GOV*'s office to ask if I would support an amendment to allow publicly funded gubernatorial candidates to raise $200,000 more in the general election than the law currently allows, an obvious advantage for incumbents.

Absolutely not, I told them, putting on my own best good government demeanor, which is pretty much the same as the men's, minus the tie and the fly problem. I railed about campaign finance reform that only ended up allowing candidates to spend more money. Clearly, they didn't want anyone railing on the floor.

At the same time, we put in an amendment to make all multi-client lobbyists political committees, meaning none of them could bundle more than $500 per candidate. This caught the attention of men on both sides of the aisle. Officeholders in Washington have far more sources of money than in the states. They may be able to live without bundling. Michigan men didn't really think they could, but voting against the amendment would be deadly.

So here was the situation on the House floor: women were unhappy about killing off *EMILY's List*, lobbyists were unhappy with our amendment, male colleagues were unhappy about unhappy lobbyists, and the *GOV* was unhappy about his $200,000. What's a boy to do? Cave in. They agreed to remove all the *EMILY's* List language and we agreed to withdraw the lobbyist amendment and support their $200,000.

So we won.

For about a week.

When the bill arrived back in its chamber of origin, the Senate *DOOFUSES* retained the *GOV's* $200,000, but also reinserted the *EMILY's List* language with the House committee's later starting date. Their explanation was that having already taken the heroic and difficult step of passing blatantly sexist legislation in the open (they didn't refer to it as "blatantly sexist"), they simply couldn't back down. It would make them look like fools. (As if they needed any help in that.)

> "You've come the wrong way, baby."
> —*EMILIO's List*

When the bill returned to the House for approval of the Senate language, I quickly pointed out to the representatives from the *GOV's* office that we had made a deal. How could this have happened?...I wondered out loud. The *GOV*, after all, controls everything the Senate does, up to and including their bathroom habits. My, my, the *GOV's* office commiserated with me, they just did everything they could, short, of course, of keeping their end of the bargain. After all, they had their $200,000.

By the time the House acted again, someone (surely not anyone from the *GOV's* office?) had quietly managed to scare the hell out of some anti choice Democratic men, warning them that they were certain to be on *EMILY's* hit list in their 1994 primaries. That was totally false since *EMILY's* focus is almost solely on federal and statewide offices. But so strong was the *FOE* and so weak-kneed the opposition that the strategy worked. *EMILY's List* lost by one *VOTE*.

"Good things come to those who wait and wait and
wait and wait and wait and wait and wait and wait
and wait and wait."
—*EMILIO's List*

Perhaps the saddest part of this whole story was
the acquiescence of all of the House's pro choice
Republican women, albeit apologetically from two of
them. They chose to hide behind the phony mantle of
taxpayer protection and senate rights to protect their
current *GOV's* $200,000. But in taking the "Yea,
Team!" route, they also eroded the fundraising potential of any pro choice Republican women who might
want to run for *GOV* in the future with the help of
WISH List.

Looking back, women probably made two mis-
takes in all this. The first was forgetting that the rules
process is the most powerful in any political setting
and men always control the rules. As soon as women
figure out the rules, men change them. So rules related
to raising money, the father's milk of politics, must
change as soon as women figure out how to use them.

The other mistake women made was designating
1992 as The Year of the Woman, instead of something
like The First Annual Year of the Woman. Men took the
title at its face value and they were graciously willing to
give us one year out of 216. Wanting two or even more
Years of the Woman was asking a bit much. And we
did, after all, call it The Year of the *Woman*, not *Women*.

In the meantime, rumor now has it that the Sons of

Everyman, a newly formed group which includes about 90 percent of the male members of the Michigan legislature, has introduced a legislative resolution asking that the east (or right) wing of the Capitol in which *EMILIO*'s wisdom was found be named after their forebear and mentor. They want to call it Everyman's House.

"'Government cannot exist half-slave and half free.'
It can, however, exist all male."
—*EMILIO's List*

"Don't get mad. Get elected."
—*EMILY's List*

[11]

REFLECTIONS ON
THE SPERM POSSE

Just when we were wondering if The Year of the Woman was over, we found out that it never began.

Thanks to those daring young men whose flies open with ease in Lakewood, California, thousands of us who worked so hard to add four women to the United States Senate in 1992 soon discovered that the Spur Posse's "victory" total—in some cases individually—was far greater than ours. In fact, if you total all of the women in Congress, we're still behind.

Here's how it worked. Each young man scored a point every time he scored with a different young woman. Was it supposed to be a secret? Hardly. Private scores would prove nothing.

How did this happen? Or how did it not stop happening? Men today are supposed to be more sensitive about women as individuals and the younger generation was to make the real difference in gender equality. But these please-don't-tell-me-they're-atypical young men in California view women only as bodies to be conquered. And if in a moment of perverted grace we're willing to forgive some defective masculine gene, how can we possibly justify the attitude of the young women involved? The typical response of many, though not all, of them was a shrugged "Everybody does it." Or, more to the point, "Every *body* does it."

So who's at fault?—if you even think something's wrong with all this. Sure, blame the liberals. After all, aren't "teenage sex" and "left wing conspiracy" almost synonymous? But let's get real. Who controlled the legislative, educational, social and cultural agenda in America from 1980 to 1992, beginning at a time when even the oldest of the Spur Posse were still prepubescent? You got it. These are Ronald Reagan's boys. These are George Bush's boys. These are Rush Limbaugh's boys. *Ad nauseum*: The Sperm Posse.

Before you pass this off as the wild ranting of another feminazi, see if anything below sounds familiar.

THE RIGHT WING MALE'S GUIDE TO SEX FOR BOYS

First, you have to understand women. Women's only role in society is to have babies.

Now for us guys.

It's absolutely natural to chase skirts, wolf-whistle, ogle and leer. Don't be put off by people who criticize you for it. We're born with it.

It's also perfectly normal to use vulgar language around the guys. Not around the girls. But, hey, if they hear it, whose fault is that? Yours?

Always remember, follow nature and abstain from condom use until you're at least eighteen.

A word about AIDS. It's your fault if you get it.

Finally, don't listen to anything you hear about sex from your teachers at school. Ask your friends instead.

Oh, and don't touch your thing.

THE RIGHT WING MALE'S GUIDE TO SEX FOR GIRLS

Women's only role in society is to have babies. If you have a problem with this, your mother is probably a lesbian, you're probably one yourself and you can skip the rest of this lesson.

Now to understand the guys, which is the most important part.

Men pursue women naturally, instinctively and aggressively. Women who try to stifle these tendencies are responsible for all the gay men in America.

Always remember: follow the man's lead and never keep condoms around. They inevitably lead to pregnancy.

A word about AIDS. It's your fault if you get it.

Finally, don't listen to anything you hear about sex from your teachers at school. Ask your friends instead. Or just follow the guy's lead.

Oh, and save it for marriage.

So there we were, progressive women spending

the 1980s conscientiously teaching basic human decency, mutual respect and self-respect to our children—what The Year of the Woman was really all about. And there they were, absorbing political sound bites and talk radio.

Perhaps this shouldn't come as a surprise since the political rising tide of progressive women and the political rising tide of conservative right wing males happened concurrently in this country, beginning around 1980. While the parallel origins of these marches toward power were probably coincidental, each side now promotes itself as the logical answer to defeating the goals of the other.

All of this, of course, plays itself out in the legislature. Progressive women accuse right wing men of robbing our bodies, forcing their religious beliefs down our throats and allowing epidemics of teenage pregnancy and AIDS to go unchecked because of their hypocritical views of sex. They accuse us of murdering babies, insidiously indoctrinating their children with dangerous liberal beliefs and causing epidemics of teenage pregnancy and AIDS through our deceitful feminist role in fomenting the sexual revolution.

If you're keeping score, both the Spur Posse and the Sperm Posse continue to hold a wide lead. Our bills almost never pass. Theirs almost never fail. In fact, the most exciting victories I can remember in the legislature were the extremely rare occasions when we actually defeated one of their initiatives. We win by not losing.

Which makes me wonder if there ever really was a Year of the Woman.

It couldn't have been 1992. Thanks to the Spur Posse and their mentors, that was the Year of the Male Boob.

[12]

WHERE'S WALDA?

A Reader's Guide to the Women of the Legislature

Don't you just love those shows that feature elected women, hold them under microscopes, impale them on pins, so that viewers can find out what women legislators are like? "How Immigration Affects Congress." "Killer Bees Make It To The Potomac!"

The programs serve no purpose. They almost never discuss issues. Male legislators are invited on to study foreign policy, the budget, health care. Women legislators are invited on to be studied. "Look!" show hosts shout. "Look what we found! Isn't this peculiar? Let's find out what they're like. Are these gals different from their male counterparts or what?"

Well of course we are. Anatomy counts for something. For example, it takes us longer to use the lavatory facilities. It's a real problem on days when votes are coming hot and heavy for hours at a time. Votes always seem to be spaced to allow men to whip in and out of the legislative men's room, but unless a woman is running the session, women either have to suffer or miss votes.

This became a particular sore point after Michigan had renovated its House chambers, including both lavatory facilities. For some reason, the lavatory remodeling was done before remodeling the rest of the antechamber which then necessitated tearing out the all-new women's lavatory facility and moving it. In one of those great, historic, legislative victories, women legislators won the right to share time in the men's lavatory (they on the hour, we on the half hour—which we also used to decorate the urinals with flower decals), rather than having to climb two flights of stairs to use the next closest facility during the second remodeling. The press had a field day with the women's bathroom problems, but none of them ever wrote a story questioning why the men in charge of renovations had wasted thousands of dollars on remodeling the same lavatory twice.

But other than anatomy, which also makes us easier to find—few men wear floral prints—the answer to the talk show question of whether women legislators are different than men is simple: No.

As much as I hate to snatch away the only reason we're ever invited on these shows, it's the truth. We are not different. At least not in the way most men would have the public believe. In fact, being considered different wouldn't be a problem if men weren't the ones in control of defining us. They create a world view that presents some serious difficulties for elected women.

First, if we really are different, then just a few of us are more than enough, like insuring a certain percentage of people from each state or region of the country. We didn't run for office to provide variety.

Second, if women are different, do we think and act monolithically? Hardly. Men who refuse to look at us as individuals think that. Some fear it. They see us as a faceless band of marauders invading their mental landscape with our ideas. It's just not true. Some of us are very liberal, some very conservative. The differences among ourselves make us more valuable, more legitimate—less different, actually.

On the other hand, those disagreements we do have among ourselves pose special problems, not because we can't handle them, but the press can't. Elected men are supposed to disagree. But if every woman except one in the legislature agreed on an issue, the story in the paper the next day would be "Women Split on Issue." Worse, many of our male colleagues would seize the headline and use it to ignore our interests and demands.

Third, being different almost always implies that women only care or care more about domestic issues. Wrong. Women *think* more about domestic issues. If we were the only ones who cared about them, there would be, for example, no family leave law in this country. Granted, it took years to come to fruition, but it did pass. Many of my male colleagues are wonderful fathers, have working wives, experience the same kinds of child care problems that the rest of the population does. It's just that it took women in Congress and state legislatures to shove the issue in front of their faces as a national problem with serious economic implications. The public already knew it. Women legislators forced men to make the connection.

The same is true for women's health. Most men care equally about it but only think about it individually, if, for example, someone they love is afflicted with breast cancer. We think about it collectively. Ergo, no women, no attention, no laws.

So it is true that we bring a new and much needed different *perspective* about issues which personally impact women more than men, but we care and think no differently about them. Or any other issues, for that matter. It is men, not women, who coined the phrase "women's issues."

Those who would argue otherwise doom women legislators to years of toiling only on domestic issues, and while they are critically important, they are not the power issues in the legislature. How many women chair or even serve on budget committees? How many women serve on foreign affairs or military committees in Congress? In the eyes of most of the press and public, particularly during elections, these are the issues to watch. These define the *real* leaders. Even when there is no foreign threat, the country's turn to domestic issues means the economy in general, not hungry children. Whether that is appropriate or not doesn't matter. The important thing is that it's true.

Fourth, if women are different, are they less partisan than their male colleagues? No. We do, after all, come into office as Democrats or Republicans. When I was first elected, I hoped that wasn't true, that women could coalesce on issues much more easily than men. To some extent, we can and do. But while far fewer women than men are willing to jump off a partisan cliff for the cause, the truth is that we're almost never asked to. What we do is of far less interest to our respective caucuses, parties or party support groups because we simply aren't players. As we become players, that sometimes changes. I've seen it happen. Some women who come into a powerful position change markedly from an attitude of "let's all try to work this out together" to "my party, my Governor, my life." As disappointing as that is, it's a fact of political life.

Fifth, if women are different, are they less politically ambitious than men? No. In my political salad days, I used to say that the one thing that separated political men from political women was that politically active men, whether in office or not, were nothing more than walking erections; lacking the required appendage, women simply functioned differently. I was wrong. Whatever the female counterpart to a walking erection might be, we have some both in and out of the legislature. People who only enter politics to enhance themselves act the same way, no matter what their gender. And people who want to succeed to higher office have little choice but to bump everyone else out of their way, no matter what they're using for bumping. Remember, we didn't make the rules, but we have to live by them.

Sixth, if women are different, are they more honest than men? No. While I can think of few women with whom I have served who have ever displayed an iota of dishonesty, and can think of plenty of men who have, the papers have told stories of women who took bribes, of women who abused their office for their own benefit. And I've encountered a few politically active women outside the legislature who could most generously be described as scumbags. If we abuse power less, it's because we have less power to abuse—and because we perceive power differently.

So assuming men, with a little prodding, care equally about the same issues, and assuming women are equally partisan, equally ambitious, perhaps equally dishonest, why bother electing women?

This is the point at which women's definitions come into play.

First, we simply have a right to be there. If legislatures are to be representative bodies, everyone should be represented.

Second, we do force discussion on issues that would otherwise be neglected.

Third, while elected women may be pushed around plenty within the legislative framework, most women are far tougher to push around on issues than most men. It's really quite understandable. Women

who achieved elected office went through far more tri-
als of fire than almost any of their male colleagues. In
addition to proving themselves as legitimate candidates, these women often had to first prove themselves as legitimate people. For us, anatomy does not
equal qualifications.

So the overwhelmingly male lobbying corps,
which usually ignores us anyway, often finds that
women are far harder to waver. Having come into
office by routes with which most men simply can't
identify, we are hardly about to leave those routes for
someone else's agenda.

Of course, there are certainly scattered examples of
women caving in when things get tough—a few really
disappointing. And yes, I have served with a small
number of women who could never be accused of trying to outsmart their male colleagues, basically
because they had nothing to outsmart them with. We
have our Rhinestones too. More senior women try to
help, but it's not always possible. So we just shake our
heads and move along.

Interestingly, every one of the women in this small,
sorry group was carried or pushed into the legislature
by a strong man—a former boss, another legislator, a
lobbyist. This male mentor wanted to make sure he
had someone there to do his bidding or to carry on his
own sometimes twisted traditions—and a woman
would suffice if he couldn't find a man to do it. With
little idea of why they even ran for office, it's understandable why these women can't cope. Ultimately,

once in the legislature, they are ignored by men and shunned or intimidated by women. I feel sorry for them. I feel sorry for us.

One strong woman colleague refuses to associate with weak women at all. While I share her concerns, the truth is that many of our male colleagues have even fewer qualifications and nobody seems to mind having them around. But it's a bigger problem for us. Since we are all viewed as a group, we are all representative of one another. If one woman is a jerk, many think we all are. Our weak sisters weaken all of us. On the other hand, weak males don't weaken their male colleagues since their very maleness qualifies them for office. If all but one of the men in the legislature suddenly became comatose (of course, some already are), the one man left standing wouldn't consider it a reflection on him or his gender. Neither would the press or public.

But rather than being weak, intimidated, or comatose, it is far more likely that women legislators will be aggressive, will push hard on issues, will take an "in your face" position when necessary. That sort of stance is not beloved by many of our male counterparts, even though they do the same. I've done it now and then, and I can remember placing my shaking head in my hands as I watched some women go not one, but ten steps too far with some of our male colleagues. "She's really asking for it," I groan.

That's when I have to wake up and remind myself that we have every bit as much right to be there as the men do and that I am falling victim to the "battered woman legislator syndrome," in which we believe that the negative, sometimes obnoxious reactions of particular male colleagues were brought on through some fault of our own. These men slash and burn their way through the agenda while we are expected to tip-toe silently through the chambers. They confuse us with wives. Worse, they confuse us with vestal virgins. Our challenge is to remember that we are neither.

Fourth, in spite of our flaws and idiosyncrasies, most women do run for office with an agenda other than just winning office. Our perception of power is not the power itself, a common thread among most of our male colleagues, but how to use that power to effect change. That's a real asset for the public.

Fifth, because we know we are at a sometimes psychic and always numerical disadvantage, we have to know our issues far better than many of our male colleagues know theirs. This becomes critical in an arena where many of our bills are ignored simply because the almost inevitably male committee chair doesn't like, doesn't relate to, or doesn't even know women members. When we get our one shot, we have to make the most of it.

Sixth, and most important, the vast majority of women bring a different perspective on government to the legislature. It is the perspective of the unempowered. Since the public generally views itself as unempowered in its relationship to government, that public can elect women knowing that we are far better able to identify with their standing, to listen to and understand their needs, to just remember that they're there.

Because our common background is inevitably one of being an outsider and because so many elected men attempt to perpetuate that once we're in office, we remain both insider and outsider forever. Few women ever forget that, no matter how powerful they become. If the public wants their government institutions to be public bodies instead of private clubs, they should elect people who fit the public mold, no matter what their anatomical mold might be.

Of course, this might pose something of a problem for the interview and talk shows. Will we be harder or easier to find as our numbers grow? Will we become undesirable as guests when we are no longer anomalies? And if invited, what ever will we talk about? Will we be deemed useful only when issues like prenatal care or women's health are on the agenda? Or will we be asked to discuss budgets and foreign policy?

The suspense is almost too much to bear.

I can't wait.

[13]

HIS WIFE

Sometimes people ask me why I do what I do, why I work so hard for choice, why I become so angry--some might say cutthroat--when I see women being mistreated or short-changed. I tell them that I do it for the next generation of women, so that they won't have to fight for their rights as we have fought, so that they will get whatever they want in life because they legitimately deserve it.

But every now and then I am reminded that millions of women came before us who had no rights and no voice and no one to speak for them. So while I hope the following words provide some benefit to the generations of the future, they are dedicated to the generations of the past.

Whenever I visit Arlington National Cemetery, I am reminded of those old lines, "In Flanders fields the poppies blow/Between the crosses, row on row." Although the words describe another place, they capture the gripping symmetry of the thousands and thousands of Arlington's identical white tombstones.

Most people who visit Arlington these days come to see the Kennedy brothers. And if they take the standard tour, they will also see the sections reserved for veterans from each of our nation's conflicts. But on a recent visit, I "toured" Arlington with a friend who lives nearby and strolls through frequently. She has found what most of us will never see. What we were perhaps never meant to see.

There are more people buried in Arlington than you think. On the back of many tombstones—who would look there?—is another inscription. It says "His Wife." That's it. His Wife. A few, *very few*, say something like "Lucy, His Wife." Almost never a date of birth or death. Buried behind Her Husband, not next to him, no tombstone of her own.

I wonder if she knew her fate, her ultimate resting place, her ultimate *legacy*. I suppose some did and simply had no option if they wished to be buried "with" their mates. But others certainly didn't and all of them deserved more than being offhandedly relegated to the back of a tombstone.

We know at least a little about Her Husband. Always, we know his first and last name, date of birth, usually his rank and any military honors he received.

And his date of death is a clue to if he died in battle. But we know nothing about her.

I wonder what she was like, His Wife. Was she widowed young by a war which she obviously did not create? Did she keep their home together, their family intact, while he went off to fight? Did she support the war? Oppose it? If she had opinions, did she keep them to herself? Did she ever get a chance to vote?

Whatever the case, the Arlington experience—a sad, angry and indelible one—has led me to view His Wife as a metaphor for all women in this country. After all the years of so-called progress, after all the years of *living*, we are still, in the eyes of far too many, relegated to the back of the tombstone.

Look at the statistics. We monopolize some fields: 94 percent of registered nurses, 75 percent of K-l2 teachers, 99 percent of secretaries, 96 percent of house-keepers and child care workers. Eighty percent of working women are employed in a narrow range of twenty of the lowest paying occupations and the male-dominated vocational programs, both public and private, continue to channel women into training for those jobs. Our very numbers in all of these fields make us almost invisible: when you can't see the forest for the trees, you generally don't notice the individual trees either.

In most occupations, though, our numbers are so small that we are almost literally invisible: we represent 15 percent of architects, 9 percent of engineers, 2 percent of airplane pilots, 20 percent of doctors, 21 percent of lawyers and judges combined, 33 percent of teachers at the college and university level (only half full time), 11 percent of college and university presidents, 16 percent of police officers, 3 percent of firefighters, 8 percent of clergy, 10 percent of the members of Congress. The number of women on corporate, professional, civic, or charitable boards is miniscule and they are recycled and replaced by one another whenever there is a "woman's vacancy."

Some might claim that I make too much of our collective invisibility, but the 1992 report by the Women, Men and Media Project at the University of Southern California confirms that reading the paper is not unlike a stroll through Arlington. Although we represent over half the population of this country, only 13 percent of the names mentioned on the front pages of twenty large newspapers used in the study were women. Not invisible? Men have two thirds of the bylines and three quarters of the opinion pieces on the op ed pages. It will therefore come as no surprise that less than 10 percent of the nation's editors are women.

It should also come as no surprise, then, that we almost never even found out about Anita Hill. The Senate and their staff knew about the charges more than a month before they became public, President Bush and his staff at least three months before. Can't you hear the conversations? "A sexual harassment charge? Just throw that one on the back of the tombstone." But one senate staffer, bless him or her, refused to shut up and forced everyone else to look.

Just as that small percentage of women in Congress finally forced their colleagues and the National Institutes of Health into putting $500 million into *looking* at women, after billions and billions had been spent on men—not simply on men's diseases, but on diseases which affect both genders and in which only men were studied. Why? According to many in the once totally male-dominated National Institutes of Health, it's because we menstruate, we throw off the results. For whom?

Being accused of menstruating is probably better than being forgotten about altogether. Some years ago when I served on a committee reviewing legislation to create a state venture capital endeavor, I could not help but notice that while a number of places were assured for minorities and Native American Indians (and they always mean male minorities and male Indians), there were no such assurances for women. When I asked about the omission, I was told, "It was an oversight. We forgot." You forgot? Fifty-one percent of the population? One third of small business owners, which the program was meant to serve? An oversight?

And although I've often said that it's better to be hated than ignored, since if people hate me they at least know I'm there, I'm still not certain if being an oversight isn't a little better than being deliberately expunged. Case in point: that cinematic little gem, *The Silent Scream*, produced, misrepresented, and distorted by Right to Life, in which the only players are a fetus, a male doctor, and a teddy bear. No woman. His Wife. Whoever thought that menstruating would come to this?

Or this: for years, no woman served in Michigan's House leadership, which meant, among other things, that the thousands of schoolchildren who visited the Capitol never saw a woman running the sessions, never saw a woman in a position of authority. His Wife might well disappear among the male masses on the floor, but she is unmistakable wielding a gavel. Seeing is believing.

Finally, there was tacit agreement to allow one woman into leadership. Tokenism, however, is not only condescending but dangerous because it deliberately leaves out everyone else. And the one, always lesser spot we're given also precludes us from ever having the best spot. Like getting the back of the tombstone instead of the front.

If it is possible to pick our way through all these grim stories and statistics, what's the best avenue to increased visibility? Most think the solution lies in electing more women to public office, but that path is torturously slow. The unprecedented surge of elected women in 1992 was accompanied by an unprecedented attack from various scared male politicians on women—all of whom were identified as radical feminists, perhaps best defined as those of us who insist on our own tombstones. But in 1994, the emotions will subside, Anita Hill will be forgotten, and both parties will have come up with quietly circulated little brochures on how to defeat a woman.

Others would suggest we turn to our legislatures

and Congress for action, but their pace is at best lethargic and their total male dominance offers little hope of speeding up the process.

That leaves the courts. If we are to be invisible, let us start to haunt them. For example, the reason that fewer than half of women college faculty are tenured, compared to 71 percent of men, is that the tenure process is completely closed and almost totally controlled by old men who see no place for women in college. Let's go to court and break open the tenure proceedings. Or sue for equal health care. Or take the vocational programs to court.

The judicial system is the one place we have the right to stand up and say, "I'M HERE!" It's not a lot to ask: legal recognition, legal *visibility* of our very humanity.

Which brings us back to Arlington. After finding the tombstones, I did a little research. Originally a plantation, Arlington was willed by its owner, George Custis, to his daughter, Mary. She married Robert E. Lee, who left the estate in 1861 to join the Confederacy. Shortly thereafter, federal troops occupied the land and the government levied a property tax. Mary Lee sent an agent with the money, but it was rejected because the title holder—Her Husband—had not made the payment himself. The government confiscated the property. Perhaps we should nominate Mary Custis Lee for a wry "first": the first American woman to lose her own estate because she didn't send Her Husband to pay the taxes with Her Money.

Which brings us back to His Wife. I still don't know

exactly what we should do about her. I know we should do something. Should we erect a Tomb of the Unknown Wife? Should we petition the Department of the Army, which oversees Arlington, to provide a list of all the women buried there?: soldiers, nurses, *and* His Wife. Should we establish a His Wife Foundation to raise money to place flowers on Her Grave so that at least others will know she's there?

Short of those ideas, perhaps we can best honor His Wife through our own work. There are, after all, more than two lines to "In Flanders Fields." Part of the last stanza is equally compelling:

> Take up our quarrel with the foe:
> To you from failing hands we throw
> The torch; be yours to hold it high.
> If ye break faith with us who die
> We shall not sleep....

Let us then rededicate ourselves to justice and equality and visibility. Dedicate your next day of work—at home or in the office—to her. Dedicate your next volunteer activity to her. Dedicate your next contribution to her. If you're running for office, dedicate your campaign to her. And above all else, when you cast your vote next time, you make sure you cast it for His Wife.

EPILOGUE

Not long ago, I attended a nonpolitical meeting during which a young woman who played a critical role in the organization defiantly, even proudly, announced to the audience that she was resigning because one of the men in the male-dominated group had pointedly told her, "We don't really want any women here."

I smiled and winced at the same time. I smiled as I tried to calculate how often that, or that by inference, has been said to me during my tenure in office. After a quick roll through of eleven years, I figured I would have left the legislature about five hundred times had I reacted as she did.

I winced because she had unwittingly caved in. She had given the men exactly what they wanted: her disappearance from what they considered their exclusive group. She should have toughed it out. As I have often said, if you can't beat 'em, you can at least aggravate 'em into an early grave. It's a pretty easy technique to learn.

Other techniques are a lot more mundane, a lot less fun, but probably a little more acceptable. Just as many of my male colleagues have now come to accept my gender and learned, or at least tried to learn, to understand it, so, too, have I learned to understand theirs. Each of us has our own way of handling relationships with our male counterparts. One woman colleague, for example, attributes her success to her experience as a den mother for each of her four sons' cub scout troops. These tenuous collegial dances aren't always easy. Someone's toes are inevitably stepped on. Usually ours.

While we dance, we pray for reinforcements. They're coming, but ever so slowly. And the rush to term limitations has dealt us a serious blow. The surest way elected women can gain power is through the seniority system which, archaic though it may be in many ways, still offers us half a chance at a stronger voice. In a term-limited, male-dominated legislature— and I don't expect to see equal numbers in my lifetime—seniority will become meaningless and we will automatically lose many of the gains and most of the clout we've worked so hard for over the years.

My seniority has made the legislature a much more comfortable place for me now. The neanderthals are still there, of course, but there are fewer of them and more of us every year. Sometimes I wonder if I'm fooling myself when I'm invited into an inner circle decision meeting. I'm not sure if I'm there because they really respect me and I wield influence on a number of legislative issues, or if I'm just there because many men have become more sensitive about single-sex meetings. So one of us gets invited. I don't think that's true, but I am also acutely aware that far less senior men are easily and naturally invited in while far less senior, equally capable women remain stranded by the wayside.

But the changes are still evident. Most of my male colleagues truly want to include women, truly try very hard not to view us differently. Even though some are a little slower at it than others, they deserve credit for trying, for turning their backs on some of the still very powerful sexist overlords with whom we serve who continue to cling to their traditional weaponry. In a way, I've even mellowed a little—*just a little*—about them. They're actually a pretty sad bunch. Poor dears. The legislature appears to be the only place they can be orgasmic.

On the not so mellow days, when the verbal abuse and sexist machinations become so overwhelming, so deliberately effeminating, I've wondered whether it was worth it. I've dusted off my resume more than once. But then I remind myself that the battle over issues about which I care deeply is truly more important than the battle of the sexes into which so many women legislators have been reluctantly drawn. Or else the little suckers do something so hilariously inane that I simply can't bring myself to leave. Where else could I get this kind of sideshow?

So I laugh it off, however uneasily, and gravitate back to the legislative *mensches* to remind myself that they really aren't all alike.

Some of those *mensches* will surely read this book. I suspect, hope, that they will laugh with me and I think most will understand it. Others will be a little discomforted, but, hey, they should be grateful for all the stuff I left out.

And then there are those male colleagues who, if they even deign to look at one page, will undoubtedly use this book to justify their micro world view about the women with whom they serve: that we are obnoxious, aggressive, vengeful, ball-breaking bitches. Who ought to be someplace else.

But that's how life is under the dome. They'll just have to learn to live with it.

I did.

GLOSSARY

Commit these terms to memory if you run for office.

Anatomy: What qualifies men to run for office. See also, *Experience* (#2), *Qualifications*.

Balls: What men have—anatomically. Very good.

Ballsy: What some women are like. Very bad.

Congress: A place where men gather to set policy. Its almost exclusive male dominance accounts for the common reference to the *members* of Congress.

Convention: A political gathering together of thousands of men and a few women to figure out which men should be elected to government or party office.

Demographics: A reflection of the many different kinds of men in the country.

Equal Time: What men demand whenever women achieve something—about once a decade.

Experience: 1. What qualifies women to run for office. Many years of wide and varied activities. 2. When used in reference to a male politician, anatomy.

Feminist: Bad. Any woman who even vaguely suspects she should be treated equally.

Gender Balance: One, but not more than one, woman anyplace.

Gender Imbalance: More than one woman anyplace. See also, *Two*.

Gender Neutral: Good. For men only. See also, *Universal*. Example: Research money for prostate cancer is gender neutral.

Gender Specific: Bad. Narrow-based policy which applies only to women. Example: Research money for breast cancer is gender specific.

Legislature: See *Congress*.

Men's Issues: Anything that is not a *Woman's Issue*. See also, *Gender Neutral, Universal*.

More Than One: How many men should serve on a committee, board or commission.

One: How many women should serve on a committee, board or commission.

Qualifications: See *Anatomy, Experience* (#2).

PAC: 1. Good. A source of money for men to maintain control of every level of government. See also, *Gender Neutral*. 2. Bad. A source of money to help one woman get her toe in the door. See also, *Gender Specific*.

Phyllis Schlafly Syndrome: A solution to a male crisis: whenever men in control face huge masses of women demanding something or opposing something men are doing, the men find one woman (often, on a national level, Phyllis Schlafly herself) to take their side. This is supposed to signal to the public that women are split down the middle on the issue and therefore no one has to pay attention. The Phyllis Schlafly Syndrome, in a slightly different mode, is also commonly used by large corporations or male-dominated organizations when the public begins to question their activities. Oil spills? Let a woman explain. Lethal gasses leaking? Let a woman explain. Even that overwhelmingly phallic bastion, the National Rifle Association, is turning more and more to spokes*women*. Polling apparently shows that women can make a better case for even the most offensive activities. Why else would rapists seek out women attorneys to defend them?

Seniority: 1. What men rely on to cement their power. Number of terms required to achieve: one. See also, *Anatomy*, *Experience* (#2), *Qualifications*. 2. What sometimes, though not always, helps women to be heard. Number of terms required to achieve: ten.

Sexual Recycling: The convenient practice of using the same pool of two or three women to take single places on boards and commissions to prove the gender sensitivity of the corporation or organization. If the one woman leaves, she is replaced by one of the others in the small, exclusive group of chosen ones. Sometimes, though not always, these women become part of the pool because they are married to important men.

Shared Power: The divvying up of legislative goodies among men.

Two: Too many women anyplace.

Universal: That which applies only to men. See also, *Gender Neutral*.

Women's Groups: 1. Bad: Should have interests outside politics, like cooking: National Organization for Women, EMILY's List, WISH List, League of Women Voters, and any women's organization with the word "justice" in the title. 2. Good: Do have interests outside politics, like cooking: Concerned Women for America, Eagle Forum.

Women's Issues: Any issues that men don't care about, think about, or that do not relate directly to their anatomies, except in cases where a fetus is involved. See also, *Gender Specific*.